How to Evaluate
People in Business

Charles A. Dailey
and
Ann M. Madsen

HOW TO EVALUATE PEOPLE IN BUSINESS

The Track-Record Method of Making Correct Judgments

McGraw-Hill Book Company

New York   St. Louis   San Francisco   Auckland   Bogotá
Hamburg   Johannesburg   London   Madrid   Mexico
Montreal   New Delhi   Panama   Paris   São Paulo
Singapore   Sydney   Tokyo   Toronto

Library of Congress Cataloging in Publication Data

Dailey, Charles Alvin, date.
  How to evaluate people in business.

  Bibliography: p.
  Includes index.
  1. Employees, Rating of.   2. Promotions.
I. Madsen, Ann M.   II. Title.
HF5549.5.R3D3   1983   658.3'125   82-16233
ISBN 0-07-015087-7 (pbk.)

First McGraw-Hill Paperback Edition 1983

1234567890   BKP/BKP   89876543

ISBN 0-07-015087-7

The editors for this book were Robert A. Rosenbaum and Beatrice
E. Eckes, the designer was Elliot Epstein, and the production
supervisor was Sally Fliess. It was set in Palatino by Fuller
Typographers.

It was printed and bound by The Book Press.

Contents

v

PREFACE

Since 1970 the authors have completed a series of twenty-five research and consulting projects for large organizations, mostly corporations. We had frequent occasion to observe situations in which these organizations greatly harmed themselves by ill-advised selection or promotion. Sometimes the cost would be paid in equal-opportunity lawsuits (in which a corporation always loses even when technically winning), but most often it would be paid in lowered productivity. It seemed to us that key managers in such large organizations would benefit by skill training in judging people.

The more recent of these projects brought another facet of the problem of good judgment into view, and it now appears that this second facet, the corporate system of judging, is at fault because of the waste of talent in big organizations. And so we decided to search our research files, with their data on several hundred managers and engineers, to see what could be said to improve both aspects of judging people:

- The corporate system of judging which defines the values, criteria, and evidence to be judged in hiring, promotion, and general deployment of talent

- The individual's skills within that system, especially in making judgments of other people's performance and potential

Over the last several years we have concluded investigations for twenty-five organizations, analyzing various human-resource problems. The most typical problem was how to improve promotional systems. We cannot thank our creative collaborators in those organizations without betraying confidences, but it is important to note the diversity of their fields:

Manufacturing	8	Construction	1
Government	7	Religious orders	2
Food processing	2	Colleges	2
Insurance	1	Energy	2

In both the public and the private sectors, emphasis was upon either managerial or professional work. Middle and upper management dominated the levels on which our projects were conducted, with salary ranges from $12,000 to $125,000 in industry and from $8,000 to $38,000 in government. The number of persons surveyed was 819. Data-gathering sessions varied from a half day to several days per person.

Our informants included whites, blacks, males, and females. Should these groups be judged differently? Our present view is this:

Flexibility in data gathering is desirable in equal-opportunity–problem situations. This is provided by our "written account" methods (in which the judge does not even know the gender or the race of the informant). Written accounts are flexible in that they are open-ended. The reader will find that flexibility is a marked characteristic of critical incidents, annual reports, and other accounts. This flexibility permits a disadvantaged person to present special background qualifications in his or her own way.

However, this flexibility cannot extend to the analysis of data. All groups should meet the same ultimate standards: performance results. No black runner wishes to be scored on a different time clock from that of a white runner. What about women? In very high-level jobs such as we are concerned with, there is a strong argument for using the same standards to evaluate everyone. For example, who would want to say that Golda Meir was "a great national leader, for a woman"? That would be condescending. She is to be judged on the same standard as Begin.

What kinds of conclusions can be reached from such informants as ours? Can we say that the twenty-five organizations and several hundred persons are representative of managers, professionals, and engineers generally? This is not a problem; we will not be reporting statistics since this is not a research book. But we *will* consider our own observations in the light of very numerous research studies about the validity of performance ratings and interviewing in particular. From that considered analysis, we will offer some principles and recommendations to organizations wishing to improve their judging systems.

For that reason, the many illustrations in the form of disguised, rewritten cases shown as Case 4–1, Case 4–2, and so on, are presented as examples and not as typical cases or as proof. The only proof can come when a particular organization tries out a recommendation to see if it will work.

Is our approach too open-ended? This serendipity has the great advantage of allowing us to hear the unexpected from an informant. For example, we interrogated urban social workers about what they meant by success or failure in their work. A chief preoccupation was not their clients but those in authority with whom they did daily battle in their agencies.

This ability to arrive at unexpected findings is one of the

virtues of the method of open-ended written accounts. An example of such an account is John Flanagan's "critical incidents," a robust, fundamental method in the study of human performance. When we ask for such an account, we listen for the unexpected and do not limit the answer, as do those who use questionnaires and opinion surveys. This listening makes our method humanistic. But then we use standardized content analysis, which gives our method some discipline and structure.

No approach protects anyone totally from bias. For example, we undertook the projects to answer organizations' questions about hiring, promoting, productivity, morale, or turnover. Thus we were "biased" toward serving the interests of those organizations. You will find that a frequent term in this book is "results," and one bias we do have is that results in work are important to the worker as well as to the organization.

Is this a book about personnel? We would say that it is not. The reasons are:

- The clients were line managers.

- The methods were not conventional personnel methods.

- The conclusions are far from personnel orthodoxy. We suspect they are closer to the thinking of many line managers.

Last, is there a theory behind the book? From that source of bias, we are free. First, no one theory of managing persuades us. But if we had to choose, it would lie somewhere between the viewpoint of Studs Terkel, a very human view, and that of Peter Drucker, who orders management phenomena around the concept of results. These two extremes, the utterly spontaneous and the soberly economic, are both embraced by our conception of human nature. Judging systems ought to be built around this conception of human nature. At present they are *not*.

Waltham, Massachusetts   *Charles A. Dailey*
                                            Ann M. Madsen

How to Evaluate
People in Business

1

THE CORPORATE
JUDGING SYSTEM

This book started out to show how managers can judge and be judged. The research and state of the art of judgment seem timely for offering that kind of help to corporations, for which bad judgments are especially costly.

What we found, however, in reviewing our findings in projects involving about 800 managers and professionals, was that the problems of judging their performance and potential were nested within a larger set of problems. It is still clear that judging is a priority skill worth a major effort to define and improve, but this skill can be improved only if one makes sure that the system delivers data worth judging.

We will begin by considering the individual's judgments and then show how they nest within the broader system. According to our observations, any large organization influences judgments of fitness and promotability through somewhat unconsciously ordained systems. You, the individual, perhaps "inherit" these systems, so it seems worthwhile to show how they affect your judgment in practical situations. First, we will consider your skill as an individual.

Most people believe they have good judgment of others. It is rare that anyone admits having bad judgment: it would be like saying, "I have a poor sense of humor," a remark no one makes. But most of us admit to an occasional lapse in judgment, and all of us can see that the problems following miscalculation about people are immense. It is easy to see that judging individuals—whether at work or in social, family, professional, or public life—is a critical skill. It is in fact a critical *set* of skills. One would expect a set of skills vital to the conduct of business or even of life to be of great interest to educators. However, these skills are neglected. Years are devoted to instruction in how to calculate with figures, and not even an hour to calculating about people.

Is judging people less important, and less teachable, than using numbers? But perhaps we exaggerate. Try this simple exercise:

- Make a list of the five most important decisions you have made in your career or your personal life, or both.

- Classify each decision as to whether it required you to judge a person. That is, to make the decision, you needed to know the motives, abilities, or situation of another person.

The following decisions often appear on such lists: choosing a career, getting married, choosing a college with one's son or daughter, going into business with a partner, abandoning a relationship, deciding what to do about an elderly parent. If you are like most list makers, at least half of your decisions involve judging a person. On most lists, more decisions involve judgment of people than use of mathematical skills. This is not to say that mathematics is unimportant; it is almost of supreme importance. What do we think, then, of the importance of good judgment? And, how well did your education prepare you for judging? The first time you serve on a criminal jury or face an impasse with a boss, you will see how little prepared you are.

We digress here to consider the belief of many managers that they learn about people when they study the behavioral sciences. They do acquire knowledge *about* people. It is a knowledge like that of the ardent fan who knows about football, golf, or tennis. It is not like the knowledge of the professional player. A musician, artist, or electrician has knowledge *of* rather than knowledge about. Polanyi (1958) wrote about the concept of tacit knowledge. It fits here. The judge who makes decisions well has tacit or silent knowledge, while the behavioral scientist is qualified by formal knowledge to talk about decisions.

We can hardly argue against the study of the behavioral sciences, but they do not teach judging skills. Nor do courses in logic, history, or literature directly instruct in them. Perhaps good judgment (popularly termed "people reading") is beneath the dignity of the college curriculum. Not so: every tyrant in history and every bad United States President came to power through someone's misjudgment of character.

Perhaps good judgment is not as teachable as mathematics. Robert Maynard Hutchins properly insisted that not everything "relevant" is therefore teachable. At one time, this would not have been a bad argument against teaching good judgment. However, we are encouraged by recent findings to do so. This book will not focus on research, but research makes it possible to write the book now, because it shows that good judgment can be identified and measured. For example, the component results have been found to be (Warr and Knapper, 1968, pp. 5–15):

- Evaluative or emotional judgment: to express how a person attracts, repels, or is valued by us

- Episodic judgment: to size up the meaning of a person's actions during a particular event or episode

- Personal (that is, dispositional) judgment: to estimate someone's potential accomplishments

In working out ways for you to improve your judging skills, we have noted that both intellectual and emotional aspects are reflected. In making sense of what a person is doing in a particular event, for example, the intelligent aspect of our judgment is reflected in our desire to be right about that person, to be accurate.

The emotional aspect is reflected in the empathy (or its opposite, prejudice) that we develop through observation of that event.

The word *skill* suggests practical application. The good judge is a decision maker about practical situations. We will be concerned primarily with the use of skills in four decision situations:

- Judging the causes of performance on the job
- Judging potential in the hiring interview
- Judging promotion potential
- Judging one's own career prospects

In all these, you will find the intellectual aspect of judging concerned with whether you have sufficient evidence for the decision you make. We can help you with that. You will also find it necessary to handle the emotional aspect of decision making—your own degree of openness to emotional evidence. It is harder to acquire that aspect of judgment through reading a book.

The four decision situations have weighty practical consequences; there are risks from poor decisions. These situations are not simple. The fascination of judgment lies partly in its intricate nature.

The underlying similarity of the four judging situations is a common requirement for accurate calculation. Everyone you meet gives signals through dress, gesture, and expression about his or her intentions, taste, and readiness for conversation, as is well known in dating bars. The book stands are full of treatises on how to read the signals. These books are interesting and merit your attention, but they soft-pedal the question of how you can tell whether you are reading signals correctly. They are unconcerned with validity. Against what cold, factual reality can you check your judgments for sizing up not only the new acquaintance but also the old customer—the patient who often sues for malpractice, the problem daughter, the wild son, the wayward spouse, the embezzling partner, or any fascinating character on your particular stage? People reading is as intriguing as it is necessary.

But people-reading books leave out not only the problem of knowing when your conclusions are valid, but something more—empathy. To calculate without caring is dangerous. The science of judgment is a compassionate one. You will think that we have forgotten this, amid the book's early chapters that emphasize how judgment works to secure good business results through the efforts of people. But empathy will arise through the kind of data you use as the basis for judgment. It will not receive a separate chapter because this will not be needed. Accurate judgment grows out of empathy-producing accounts of human performance.

GOOD JUDGMENT DEFINED

Good judgment means being right about a person. This means reconstructing the causes of observed performance, and it means estimating a person's future performance. These two directions of judgment require facts but make different uses of them. To reconstruct the causes of performance means to start with known results and work backward to arrive at the causes of those results: what the person or environment did to produce those results. Estimating future results starts with what the person is known to do and works *forward*. The criterion of accuracy differs in these two directions of judgment. In working backward, we can do no more than compare our reasoning with that of other qualified observers. But in working forward, since we are making a prediction of future events, we can confirm or disprove our estimates. This distinction provides the clue to the proper design of training for better judgment.

Improvement of Evaluative Judgment

Good judgment results in a value judgment. In the case of backward reconstruction, or judging the causes of performance, this means starting with the valued output of what a person does and determining how the output was achieved. In that sense we learn to evaluate a person's actions. In the case of forward reconstruction, or estimating the potential to perform, we start with known actions and estimate future values. In that sense, again, we learn to evaluate a person's actions. The point is: there is no way to exclude evaluation from good judgment, but it is necessary to control evaluation. In general, our recommendation is to let the performer take part in the reconstruction of performance, in such a way that the performer can freely express perception of the situation and help reconstruct what happened. Such a procedure will make empathy possible, although nothing will guarantee empathy. It will also make prejudice unlikely, although, again, nothing may totally exclude prejudice, since judgment, as shown above, is inevitably concerned with how we place values on people's performance.

Improvement of Episodic Judgment

Good judgment of a particular event starts with its valued end result and works back to see how this result was attained. This requires both detailed accounts of the event and detailed reasoning about it. This process is improved by (1) enriching the data we have about the event, whether it was an accident, labor grievance, sale, clever invention, or other important event, and (2) comparing our reasoning with that of other qualified judges. One of those qualified judges is the chief performer in the event.

Improvement of Personal Judgment

Good judgment of the many events making up a person's career provides the basis for estimating future values. This requires both detailed accounts of that person's past experience and reasoning from those accounts to the future. The process is improved by enriching those accounts, so that reasoning is possible, and providing feedback to the judge confirming or denying the judgments.

How One Learns

Each of the improvement programs briefly described above contains these learning mechanisms or components:

- Improving the data you have about a person to satisfy the key test question, "Do I have this person's viewpoint on what happened?" Obtaining this feedback relates the judge to the performer, thus improving empathy.

- Comparing your reasoning with that of others who have evaluated the same data. Obtaining this feedback makes for commonsense judgment.

- Comparing your estimates of the future with the factual outcomes estimated. Obtaining this feedback improves the validity of judgment.

These are all different forms of "knowledge of results" (KR). KR is the way people learn almost any skill: improving golf strokes, tennis games, handwriting, memory, and many more skills too complex to explain in a few words. In brief, three types of KR are required to improve judgment: KR-1 checks your empathy; KR-2, your common sense; and KR-3, your predictions. In any deskside program you set up to improve your judgment of people, you will need to provide yourself with all three KRs.

THE CORPORATE JUDGING SYSTEM

Thus far the manager has been treated as a solitary learner. In fact, none of us works in an organizational judging vacuum. Now we are ready to scale up our thinking, to see the tasks of judging in a broader system.

To do this, think of judging not people but their performance. Even with our scope narrowed from people to their performance, the question is still complex enough to be challenging: "What is performance, and why does it occur?" Courage to face that complexity well repays the risk. The dividends will be several orders of magnitude larger than self-improvement.

Every manager keeps book and runs a score-keeping operation. This is true in so many different ways that it hardly needs illustrating: from expense and income reports to the vastly more subtle books kept on such as the innovative results flowing from the department. Managers both keep their own scores and have scores kept on them ("What do they think of me?"). It seems a political necessity for the manager to know how score is kept above and outside the department. Much of the office gossip and the rumor mill have to do with today's changes in managers' stock within the corporation. Who's "in" or "out" is vital information. In self-defense, if not for more worthy reasons, managers should study the score-keeping operation as it is being conducted and consider how it should be handled.

While we will not concentrate on seamy office politics, it inevitably intrudes on any neat rational scheme describing the process of performance. We will start with such a rational scheme incorporating many different research perspectives (without, it is hoped, bogging managers down in the minutiae which interest professional behavioral scientists). Such a scheme is the "micromap," or miniature picture of performance. The micromap is drawn to show the varieties of judging skill and score keeping and how they are interrelated.

RESEARCH IN ATTRIBUTION

We pause for a research input, one of the few in this book. This example may clarify why human performance is so hard to make sense of and to influence. Think about this example, again, when you read Chapter 2.

In the "attribution" experiment, which tries to discover why people see different causes in the same behavior, a typical finding shows interesting differences between the performer and persons observing. For example, a performer is asked to solve a puzzle made up of blocks to be assembled on a table. The performer makes an attempt and is then asked to account for what happened. An observer witnessing the entire proceeding is also asked to account for what happened. One consistent finding is that the performer tends to discuss the specific "local" facts about the situation—materials provided to work with, the possibly misleading instructions, and points at which the performer broke through the obstacles to get the job done. What does the *observer* talk about? Observers make broader inferences (attribute "distal" qualities) about the performer's style and ability—creativity, intelligence, persistence. That is, a boss, coach, or other observer will "see" enduring qualities which show through the worker's specific performance. In brief, the performer talks about concrete action and the observer about persisting traits. This will be true whether the observer supervises the worker or not. At least, this is the implication of the research published so far.

A particular example may clarify further some reasons for the worker's local ("proximate") perception and the observer's distal perception. In a research project, videotapes of each worker's performance were made:

- One tape was shot directly across the table, facing the worker and recording the performance.

- The other was taken over the worker's shoulder, recording the same performance.

The two videotapes were shown to observers who were not physically present at the actual performance to illustrate the effect of the vantage point. What kinds of causes were now attributed?

1. The "opposed" videotape observer attributed distal qualities of ability and effort.

2. The "over-the-shoulder" observer attributed performance characteristics like those seen by the worker in his or her own performance.

Are there *two* realities? The performer has, we think, too narrow a view. But this view is real. The observer has too inferential a

Figure
1-1

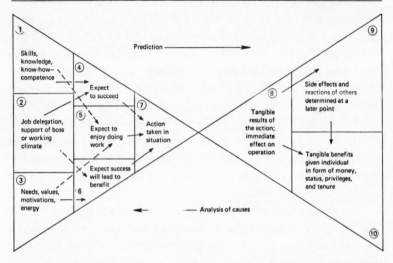

Micromap of performance, showing things judged by both an observer and a performer, or by one of them, when inferences are made about a specific episode of performance.

view. But this view may be very useful to consider. In the micromap of performance (Figure 1-1), we have combined both realities in one diagram. The immediate concrete action, for example, is concentrated in Areas 7 and 8.

THE MICROMAP OF PERFORMANCE

While judgment takes the broad forms described above, it takes much more specific forms within the manager's job. Figure 1-1 is a commonsense drawing which also fits research evidence. It describes the sequence of things done to move from inputs (people entering the jobs in the system), through action or performance

Figure
1-2

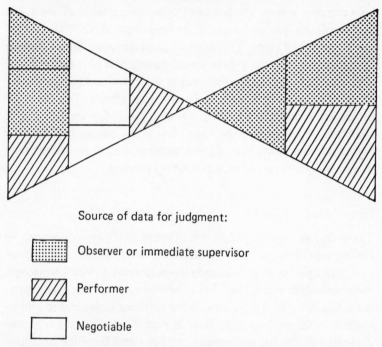

Source of data for judgment:

Observer or immediate supervisor

Performer

Negotiable

Primary sources of judgment (that is, who can make a judgment about each area).

delivered day by day, to reach eventual outputs (results or the lack of them). We are concerned with what makes a person carry out these actions and how they are effective. This is the performance process. We call the figure a micromap because it deals with single episodes, and hence with episodic judgment. Most of this book will deal with that kind of judgment, and only in the closing chapters will we move to the "macromap," or judgment of persons rather than of specific events.

What the micromap shows is a panoramic view of what we need to judge about an event, its causes and effects. This view is seen by several cameras, and the separate pictures are then spliced together for a common vision. The boss and subordinate, we shall show, see systematically different areas of the landscape. Areas 7 and 8 represent the actual event. The other areas all represent things leading up to the event (Areas 1–6) or consequences of it (Areas 9 and 10). The nature of judgment is different in each area and in the connections between areas. For example, when the effects of an event are compared with factors leading up to it, the judge receives useful feedback. Accordingly, the judge learns by connecting areas of higher number with areas of lower number. Below we explain how you as manager can ensure this learning process.

Input Areas 1, 2, and 3

These are, as labeled, judgments of preliminary resources such as ability to perform, support given by the environment, and motivation. Examples of Area 1 include the performer's skill, knowledge, communication ability, and know-how resulting from past experience. Examples of Area 2 include the working tools, budget, information, work setting, and, most important of all, the job or role delegated to the person through the boss and from the organization. Examples of Area 3 include the person's motives, which provide the energy that fuels effort. The motives are both psychological and economic. These areas of the micromap are deliberately chosen to represent the minimum inputs necessary to provide resources necessary for work. The inputs are related in a quantitative sense, in that if any *one* of the three is zero, *nothing* can logically happen. A person weighing 100 pounds would lack the ability to play professional football despite the strongest motivation. But even a player weighing 300 pounds, if lackadaisical, would not perform. An environmental support structure is equally necessary. The able and motivated player must still be sent into the game: the job must be delegated by the coach. In brief, if anyone of the three factors—ability, motive, or support—is zero, performance is impossible. We intend this not as a literal mathematical formula but only as an explanation of why the micromap starts with these three areas. There are very specific judging skills in each area. For example, judging an applicant's ability is obviously an Area 1 skill.

Mobilization Areas 4, 5, and 6

Resources are brought to the job in Areas 1, 2, and 3 but must then be mustered or mobilized through specific commitments by the employee. These are the concern of Areas 4, 5, and 6. These areas hook the resource inputs to the job to be done. Since what is hooked, or mobilized, is resources, Areas 4, 5, and 6 should relate to the inputs of Areas 1, 2, and 3. And so they do. If we combine Areas 1 and 2 (ability and environmental support), we have an expectation of success by the person (or the boss). We would label Area 4 confidence—expecting to succeed. If we combine Areas 1 and 3 (ability and motivation), we have talent, the person's expectation of getting involved in the job or task—expecting to enjoy it or to be involved. Finally, if we combine Areas 2 and 3 (environmental support and motivation), what do we get? One way to interpret this is expecting to benefit by succeeding. The person thinks, "If I succeed, I will be rewarded by the organization." These three forms of expectancy bring the person to life, encourage mobilization of resources in the pursuit of results, and, in brief, provoke action. Among the forms of judgment involved here would be judging a person's confidence level. If a good working climate exists, the worker will phrase judgments in ways such as these:

- "If I try, I can do it well."
- "If I do this work, I will enjoy it."
- "If I do this work well, I will benefit."

Action and Results: Areas 7 and 8

Thus mobilized, the person steps into a more or less difficult situation, appraises options, copes, endures, and finally succeeds or fails. This is the visible event. Its minimum structure is situation, action, and outcome. The parts of the event that the person is best qualified to describe we put in Area 7. The parts of the outcome that others (such as boss, customer, or client, who receive the person's output as an input) are better qualified to evaluate we call a result and put in Area 8. Both action and result must be monitored in any organization. But the emphasis varies: a bureaucratic or production organization will emphasize Area 7; a sales or entrepreneurial organization, Area 8. Among the types of judgment involved are the obvious ones supervisors must make: whether the proper actions are being taken and whether results commensurate with the costs of the actions are being obtained. The performer, too, makes such judgments. One of the mysteries which will concern us in our analysis of performance appraisal is why performer and boss do not more closely agree.

Consequences: Areas 9 and 10

Immediate results raise echoes in the organization: triggering action by others, getting recognition for good or bad results, eventually obtaining a promotion or other benefits. Sometimes good immediate results (a sale) are followed by bad longer-term results (for example, if to get the sale, one promises too much to a customer). Judgments made here concern organizational consequences (Area 9) and individual benefits (Area 10). The boss tends to pay attention to Area 9, and the performer to Area 10.

Feedback Loops

The judge who compares any area with an earlier area—Areas 8 and 7, for example—draws conclusions. Among the more important loops are:

- *Loop 8–7.* Comparing results with actions, we appraise the value of actions.

- *Loop 8–1.* Comparing results with ability, we decide what kinds of ability lead to success, or we can change our estimate of the individual's ability.

- *Loop 7–2.* Comparing actions with job expectations, we answer a question such as, "Is the person doing what he or she is supposed to do?"

- *Loop 8–4.* Comparing results with confidence, the performer may become more or less confident.

- *Loop 10–6.* Comparing benefits with promises, the performer may conclude, "This organization (boss) can be trusted (not be trusted)."

Preventing Performance

Rising concern for equal opportunity has provoked interest in how the members of one social group (white males, for example) influence the performance of lower-status employees of other groups (women and blacks, for instance). Getting a person into a system (Area 1) is only a small part of the total complex of forces which result in performance.

Let us suppose that an able member of a protected class enters the system. Let us say that this class consists of white male Texans, who at some future date are given equal-employment-opportunity (EEO) protection. But Texans are not liked or respected in the system. There are various ways to prevent the Texan's performance, among them lack of motivation (creating a job which does not appeal to the Texan's Area 3 needs) and insufficient job information and supervisory support (Area 2). In spite of adequate ability (Area 1), the Texan will not do well, according to the micromap, if not helped to form confident expectations (combining Areas 1 and 2 to form the commitments to action taking shape in Area 4). The system's maneuvers are mostly too subtle to prevent through legal sanctions. Still more subtle would be a strategy in which high expectations of personal benefit (Area 6) are falsely built up: let us say that the Texan produces good results (Areas 7 and 8), but the expected benefits are not delivered (Area 10). This would not necessarily result from a deliberate act of discrimination; it might well arise from a lack of information (Area 2) about what the job requires. The eager Texan might be working hard and effectively, but not on the things wanted by the boss. The Texan would get a terrible shock at the time of the annual review and reach conclusions such as "Hard work does not get respected here," or "They only reward their own," or (maybe less likely) "I am worthless." The micromap thus shows a number of ways in which performance can be prevented or caused to deteriorate as well as enhanced.

ESTIMATING POTENTIAL

While we will use the micromap in Chapters 2 through 5, one of its limitations is that it is built around short-run performance events. Earlier we spoke of longer-range, or personal, judgment. Can we "map" that as well? This map is similar except that, concerned with the many events making up a career, it does not come to a focus on a particular happening, as does the micromap. However, we can say that careers reveal two general themes, or enduring characteristics, which must be judged in order to estimate what any individual can and will be in the long run: what he or she *cares about* and what he or she can effectively *do*. These two themes (like Areas 3 and 1) are expressed in various ways. The first or more emotional theme includes motivation, effort, goals, values, and persistence. The second or more rational theme includes effectiveness, knowledge, information, know-how, skills, and access to such resources as money and influence. The macromap which depicts these processes in their interrelation is given in Chapter 8

(Table 8-1). What it maps is *lifelong* experience. The assumption is that knowing a person's experience in regard to both values and abilities gives the leading clue to future potential. We are concerned with the practical applications of this view of potential in Chapters 6 and 7.

CULTIVATING JUDGMENT

It is obvious that judgment is many-sided. Its complexity results not only from the various time spans over which it is used but also from the subtlety of people themselves. This subtlety may discourage many, but it must not discourage managers who are serious about their careers. They have too much to gain from improving their judgment (which we think possible) and too much at risk from the disasters of bad judgment (which managers well know) to leave judgment in the status of an intuitive talent which we would all like to have but cannot acquire.

SUGGESTED ACTIONS

What difference to your work and career will the foregoing make? How can you use the following chapters to get the greatest value from them? This is a skill-oriented book. And yet judging is a complex skill. So, the first thing we would counsel is a bit of patience. To earn our right to ask for patience, we must provide you with at least some assured benefits. Here are a few.

Improve Major Decisions of Life and Career

This benefit to you is almost too sweeping to believe. But earlier your analysis may have convinced you that at least half of your major decisions do hinge on your success in sizing up someone's performance or performance potential. You are naturally eager to obtain help with major decisions. In general, if you build your skills with minor decisions, you should be ready for major situations.

Learn the Score

In your own political interest find out how your corporation and upper management keep score. They have certain perspectives on what is important for you to deliver and how to know whether it is being delivered. At the very least, you must do homework on this. Some detailed suggestions are made in Chapters 2, 3, and 4.

Tell Others the Score

If you have found it helpful to know how the books are kept (and sometimes cooked), consider your subordinates' situation. Why not give them similar information on how you keep score (not on how you want to, but on how in fact you *do)?* That is a delicate question. You will get some help in Chapters 4 and 5.

Negotiate a Fairer Agreement

You are entitled to more reasonable judging systems, both the system used with you and the one you use with others. This is the subject of Chapters 2, 5, 6, and 7. Incidentally, one of the points made earlier in this chapter, in referring to the videotape study of attribution, is that observers and performers *inherently* differ. You should expect disagreement about the quality and causes of performance rather than be surprised by it. Your task of negotiating will never end.

Judge Evidence, Not Impressions

A major theme of this book is that human performance has a fascinating intricacy which deserves close observation. Why settle for casual impressions? The great masters of anything—sports, music, science, invention—are masters of detail. They do not give their work or their life a casual glance. No doubt you like to move fast and work fast. But when you get down to fundamentals—and human performance (yours or others') is surely your fundamental concern—details are worth your close, concentrated attention. If you learn to judge evidence, we can promise you certain benefits:

- *Morale.* While it is possible to become picky about what your people are doing, your concern about the specifics of their *performance results* (Area 8 in our micromap) is not picky. It is a way to increase morale.

- *Improving your own competence.* You can learn to collect the same revealing observations about your work as a manager as those we think you should make about your people.

- *Reducing bias.* If you are interested in how people are getting good or bad results and not in whether they are male or female, black or white, old or young, you are not biased (Chapters 6 and 7).

- *Getting control over your own career and life.* We hope to convince you that evidence about your work over long spans of time is well worth having and leads to self-management (Chapters 8 and 9).

GUIDE TO FURTHER INQUIRY

Readers who consider their judging skills or situation in particular need of strengthening in any one area will find theories relevant to that area in works in the Bibliography or in later chapters of this book. For example *attribution theory* (Heider, 1958) is concerned with how people attribute causes to performance. This is the backward judging process involved in reconstructing causes and goes by area, roughly 8–7–1 (an inference that the individual got results by using abilities) or 8–7–2 (an inference that the results were due not to the individual but to the support given by the boss or the environment). Attribution theory, however, does not help us to move in the other direction to estimate future performance. For that we need help from *assessment theory,* a very different subject (see Chapters 6, 7, 8, and 9). If we are concerned with the source of effort, we will use *motivation theory* to explore Area 3 and its consequences for Areas 5 and 6. *Job enrichment* is concerned with Area 5. The whole complex of problems involved in arousing a person to effort (Areas 4, 5, and 6) is the concern of *expectancy theory,* as developed by Vroom (1966) and Lawler (1973), among others. *Equity theory* especially helps us to understand why some jobs seem worth doing, and this is also the concern of Areas 5 and 6 (Homans, 1974). *Organizational theory* is in many ways concerned with the entire micromap, but until recently it paid greater attention to such areas as 2 and 9 and less, for example, to the assessment problem (especially to linking Areas 1, 7, and 8). Finally, *learning theory* was traditionally concerned with how rewards influence performance and hence dealt to a greater extent with feedback loops such as 8–7, 8–4, 8–1, 10–1, and 10–6.

2

LET'S REPLACE
PERFORMANCE REVIEW

Better judgment of performance would produce a payoff for you today. The trouble is that the old system of performance appraisal (including, for example, the annual review) cannot produce that payoff. To develop new skills, you need a new framework. What was the old framework, and why can't it work? (Maybe you believe it is working.)

The old system was built upon the concept of telling people how well or how badly they were doing, completing a personnel form which both you and the employee signed, and in general meeting the personnel department's requirements. Both you and the personnel department deserve something better—not to speak of the poor soul who probably did not want his or her "report card" in the first place.

The old system—for convenience it will be called PA-1 (for "performance appraisal one")—was designed some decades ago to provide objective ratings of production workers. The designers seem to have been bureaucratically minded staff people. In the belief that ratings either are scientific or can be made so, they asked managers to rate employees for various qualities. We propose to show you something better, for contrast called PA-2. We will not merely tinker with specific design features, such as better rating scales, but offer a design structure so distinctive as to require a system change.

Our studies show that PA-1 is not working to achieve what should be its central objective: improving productivity. This failure is obscured by the multiple goals that misguided staff specialists have attempted to build into the design. It is as if when they saw that the central objective was not being convincingly met, the advocates of PA-1 scrambled about for other reasons to continue to do what they were doing. Trying to make PA-1 work is as logical as building an engine to run on electric current when the fuel supply is gasoline. No amount of tinkering with the original engine can solve the problem.

What are we to think about the occasional organizations which seem to make PA-1 work? Such companies hold annual reviews; people, especially managers who make a strong effort to do them well, may regard them favorably; personnel departments feel justifiably proud. Our suspicion is that these organizations enjoy a favorable climate of human relations, good business conditions, and consistent support from the top. In other words, PA-1 may seem to work when major supporting conditions are present. Fair weather makes even a bad boat temporarily seaworthy. But the bad features are merely obscured. Instead, we recommend a rough-weather model. Even in fair-weather conditions, we doubt that PA-1 has really proved its essential claim of improving productivity.

A PRESIDENTIAL DESIGN

Professional personnel managers want to involve line managers in the operation of PA. We want to go further and involve line managers in the *design* of PA. Indeed, we want to go as far up the line as possible and have PA-2 designed by general management, the operating head. In that sense PA-2 is a "presidential design." If we want to know how to evaluate performance, we should not start with the situation of the production foreman who grudgingly obliges the personnel staff specialist's apologetic request to complete a simple form once a year. Instead, presidential design starts at the other end of the pyramid and asserts:

- PA-2 should be a top-down system. It should start with the reason why the organization exists, which is to achieve certain business objectives.

- PA-2 should ask how a corporation president, who is the closest, legally and logically, to the definition of organizational purpose, must have his or her own performance evaluated.

- PA-2 consists of a system for judging performance as if every employee were the manager of a profit center, a president reporting to a board of directors. It is not, however, management by objectives (MBO).

Where It Applies

Immediately, you will ask whether some jobs cannot be evaluated in this manner. Certainly, PA-2 cannot cover all cases. It does not cover improperly designed jobs, and it should not judge work for which PA-1 is doing an effective job.

How should you determine where the new system applies? Start at the top and push it down the layers of the organization until you are convinced that it has no further value or applicability. If you have already installed an MBO system, you will find that taking the system further is desirable. Although MBO has some of the qualities of PA-2, it lacks essential features needed to appraise the causes of performance. MBO, while a giant step away from PA-1, is not the final word on judging performance.

PA-2 treats as many people as possible as if they were managers. It does not say this stance can always be maintained. What is always true is that PA-1 does not apply to top management. Because of this inapplicability, most middle managers, many first-line supervisors, and exceptional employees do not respect the PA-1 report-card system. They respond to it grudgingly and without a genuine sense of profit. As McCall and DeVries state (1976), PA is "often viewed with the same enthusiasm as income tax forms."

Supervisors were given tools for controlling and improving work and, in recent years, for developing human resources. Their lack of enthusiasm for PA-1 was attributed to a lack of training, professionalism, or even intelligence. The lack of operating payoff from using PA was not usually recognized as an explanation of supervisory resistance. There was, however, a "general ambivalence toward appraisal" on the part of line managers and not a few personnel managers (ibid.). The most serious liability in using PA-1 was probably the lack of visible payoff. Experiments to prove that PA improves performance would not be difficult to undertake; we must assume that proof is unlikely, or else the more tough-minded advocates of PA-1 would long ago have offered it. Few persons have done experiments such as that of Herbert Meyer (1964) at General Electric.

A second liability has surfaced recently. Filed rating forms constitute a liability in equal-opportunity suits—a more serious hazard than employment tests pose. Any personnel rating form in a company's files is a liability if the ratings cannot be shown to be job-relevant, functional, and objective in the sense that they can be traced to evidence other than a supervisor's say-so. Liability does not end there. If the filed forms cannot themselves be shown to be good evidence, the selection procedures which depend on the ratings for their validity (What else can they depend on?) are in trouble. Vulnerability spreads from that point like a brush fire growing to be a forest fire. Many personnel actions, including compensation, firing, discipline, and transfer, are based on PA. Thus if the selection procedures cannot be proved to be fair, in the sense of being valid, subsequent personnel procedures will also lack a bench mark against which to be judged fair.

The problem of validity of traditional performance ratings, of course, predates the enactment of EEO laws. Statisticians have long scorned performance ratings as lacking both validity and reliability. Well-known phenomena such as "halo effects" mean that raters are using one favorable rating as the reason for another favorable rating. That is, there has never been much evidence for a rating. The rater merely uses one personal opinion to defend another personal opinion.

Another design problem, even in jobs for which PA-1's mechanistic and bureaucratic assumptions seem appropriate, is feedback. Just as KR provides the mechanism by which you can improve your judgment, it also furnishes a mechanism for improving almost any other skill. PA-1 was supposed to provide KR to every worker and thus, by informing the worker of what was going well, to strengthen productive behavior or, through the penalty of censure, to weaken unproductive elements in performance. But critics of PA-1, such as Vaccaro (1976) at Baxter Laboratories, speak of the futility of long delays: the annual review, with its year-long delay in providing feedback, cannot, according to learning-theory principles, provide timely, useful, or effective KR.

A final problem of design is inclusion of multiple objectives. In trying to persuade properly skeptical line managers that systematic PA is worth installing, personnel departments promised too many different benefits. The whole structure became weighted down with too many purposes. Thus PA-1 is reminiscent of the one-man band. The marvel of the one-man band is that anything happens at all. It certainly does not produce good music. On which of the musical instruments—promotion, compensation, morale boosting, setting training objectives, developing people, or just getting work done—is PA-1 supposed to perform?

If the engine won't run after two generations have tried to start it, it's time to ask fundamental design questions instead of tinkering with minor features. By tinkering, we mean, for example, setting behavioral standards while using bureaucratic forms, supplying more frequent feedback, reducing authority or becoming more participative in style, removing traits from personnel forms, improving the forms, and doing more research within the old framework of thought. Perhaps calling these changes mere tinkering is unfair. However, another metaphor certainly applies. Minor procedural improvements within PA-1 are like getting one foot in the water. It's time to dive in, to search for real change.

PA-2

The aim of performance appraisal is productivity rather than letting people know how well they are doing, documenting performance for possible future action, or developing people. However, additional benefits such as these will result from a PA system which genuinely aids productivity.

By "productivity" we don't mean working harder or showing a good attitude. These are means to an end, not the end itself. We do mean achieving the external results for which a particular job exists. These results must be visible and useful to someone other than the performer. That is, a corporate organization consists not of individuals working for themselves but of coordinated performers contributing to each other. This principle prevails all the way from the obvious point at which a salesperson sees that a customer is benefiting (the sale is an obvious result) to the less obvious point at which a data processing manager's information is clearly being used by managers who make decisions.

Areas

On the micromap (Figure 1-1), PA-2 starts with Area 8. The data for Area 8 may well be available to the performer, but according to our definition they must also be available to some other person, let us say, to the performer's immediate superior. The person qualified to judge Area 8 is someone who knows enough about the corporate organization to understand what the job is supposed to produce and when the output is satisfactory. Sometimes this person is not the immediate superior. The superior's role then is to learn how the output appears to the performer's clients. A superior who cannot do that has no way to handle PA-2. Jobs of this type would necessarily remain under PA-1.

What about a job which generates no visible results? A properly designed job does. PA-2 cannot be used with an improperly designed job. The problem becomes serious with many staff specialists. If no one can tell whether what has been done is useful to someone else, the justification for the job may be questionable. The justification may well be, "Because someone in authority wanted the job done." This may often be sufficient reason, but it does not make PA-2 possible.

The result is now rated. It is more or less valued by or valuable to someone. It may be so valuable that the client or customer cannot do without it at any price, or so valuable that the client is unwilling to get along without it but does consider its price or cost, or reasonably valuable (it is nice to have), or reasonably unvaluable (it is something the client wants but has problems with), or disliked (the client insists that unless the product or service is improved, it will be dropped). Or the client may no longer wish the product or service at all.

Up to this point the performer participates at most to a minor degree in the evaluation. But when we shift to Area 7 (what was done to produce the result), the performer is very much at the center of the evaluation. Here is where the appraiser obtains the performer's account of personal performance—telling what he or she tried to do in the time period appraised, such as the last quarter, and reporting obstacles, options, and priorities given, along with decisions made and approaches followed. Here is where the boss can't know enough to supply details and consequently, in conventional PA-1, must act as if wise while in fact ignorant. No immediate superior supplies the details for Area 7, because there are things to do besides constantly observing one subordinate. A boss who did nothing but supervise five subordinates could not know more than 20 percent of the average subordinate's activities.

The details required for a complete description of Area 7 often constitute what is called a "critical incident." The critical incident will be described in Chapter 3 as one of the key documents required for PA-2.

Loops

The comparison of Area 7 action with Area 8 results completes a feedback loop, or 8–7 in the notation system outlined in Chapter 1. A person whose action led to a good result tends to feel good or effective about that action and to want to repeat it. Such performers also feel good or effective if the boss is aware that they value the Area 8 results. If this were the only possible feedback loop, however, PA-2 would be a very thin system. Actually, many other loops are being completed at the same time. The performer is asking not only what 8–7 shows about how to operate but also the meaning of 9–8 and eventually of 10–8, 10–7, and so on. For example, in 10–9, the performer learns what others in the organization do or say as the side effect of the good or bad result he or she produced. The performer is making links back to basic attributes such as job satisfaction (10–3) and building a personal case for future identification with the job and with the boss.

At the same time, the boss or other observer of performance is making feedback links from the results. The boss, too, asks about links such as 10–8, 8–7, and 7–1. The evaluation is far more complex than a PA-1 personnel form shows. The boss goes through deliberations such as, "Well, I think the results here are good (8–7), but they are not really what I delegated (8–2): am I going to have to change the job, or is this performer out of line? And then I don't understand why I don't get good vibes from others (9–8) as to the value of the performance. How am I going to deal with those other people, or if I buy their valuation, how am I going to deal with the performer?"

PA-2 does not contend that all these feedback links are desirable or feasible. It contends, instead, that if they are omitted from, say, the annual review, the review lacks crucial conversations. If our version of PA is correct, it would explain why PA-1 (which omits most of the feedback links) seems irrelevant: it leaves too much out. It would explain why the average employee doubts that the evaluation discussed or reported is actually the evaluation being made. The groundwork is laid for people to show disrespect for the system and to mistrust each other.

What Should Be Done

Thus far, PA-2 has been described only in terms of completing the feedback loops which seem most vital to productivity. It begins with the vital loop 8–7 and goes on to explore the others concerning both performer and observer. In particular, it explores the original job delegation (Area 2). It must conclude with a new delegation. So much for the general process. But what is actually *said*?

THE SUBSTANCE OF PA-2

The content of PA-2 resembles the presidential review more than the report card. In going before the stockholders (or with still more detail before the board of directors), the president offers an annual report and a program for the following year. An annual report is a narrative of the events of a year, including the most tangible and significant results affecting the prosperity and future of the organization. It includes information on

- Profit and loss
- Sales volume for major product lines
- New products being designed or issued
- Labor relations
- Property and plant

These bench-mark results must be put in a narrative context: no one expects them to explain themselves. The *president* explains them. But no president's authority is sufficient to be convincing without facts. And no explanation of facts is understandable without a narrative context.

PA-2 demands the same substance in anyone else's accounting of performance. There is no reason why only a president must give an account. The president should require (most do require) an informal annual report from immediate staff members and all those reporting to him or her. They, in turn, should require such annual reports from all managers who are accountable to them, and so on down the echelons until the system cannot work further. At that point or in nonapplicable jobs, PA-2 is replaced by PA-1.

WHAT FORM IS USED?

Repeatedly, when asked to speak on the subject of performance review, one is asked to propose better forms. Everyone is discontented with the rating forms provided by the personnel manual. But in the PA-2 system this request is absurd. The president cannot prepare an annual report by completing a rating form, and the board of directors does not complete such a form in evaluating the president. Instead of a form, the president works from an outline.

The "form" for PA-2 at levels below the president is simplicity itself. We prefer a blank piece of paper. It is the instructions which are complex (see "Training for PA-2," later in this chapter). Even these instructions are dictated by the top-down logic of PA-2. Just as the president is accountable for producing operating results commensurate with the investment made during the year, all people appraised under PA-2 should report operating results and "investments" made by them. Investments include not only obvious costs but also time, energy, and other resources not calculated by accounting and financial people.

There isn't any form. There is only logic flowing inescapably from the obligation to give the company something in return for its investment in the individual. We have often asked managers this question: "What did the company get from you last year?" The easiest and most popular answer is usually phrased in terms of activity and effort: Area 7. This is insufficient. The answer must start in Area 8. When managers or other employees cannot start in

Area 8, there may be (1) an improperly designed job or (2) an immediate superior who has not set objectives and observed results.

WHAT IS RATED?

We will deal with this question in Chapter 3. Essentially, we reject the rating of qualities which are not the reason for the existence of the job. For example, the president is not properly rated for showing persistence, initiative, or creativity in ideas. These are not the reasons we have a president. The president is rated for accountabilities, and so should we all be, according to PA-2.

TRAINING FOR PA-2

As we decrease our reliance on bureaucratic forms, we must find another way to control the quality of PA. If there are no more report cards, then what? We must train people in PA-2. However, this training will differ radically from what has been done before, in these specific respects:

- First, performers must be trained to assert themselves, defend their records, and advocate their own plans and aspirations for the future.

- Then, supervisors must be trained to evaluate results, provide feedback at key points throughout the micromap, and "negotiate" performance (for example, see Sullivan and Meyers, 1976).

Training the Performer

We are all performers in the PA-2 system, from the president down. For all employees in jobs covered by PA-2, there should be a seminar or workshop on dealing with those over them in power. That seminar must show them how to use the micromap and general logic to defend their programs and productivity. It must also show them how to help those over them perform well—the least-covered subject in the world of management training. We have reviewed a large number of textbooks and management-training curricula without finding this topic presented, but we consider it number one in interest: how to work for an impossible boss. The subject, however, is broader than that. We would rather see it outlined to provide instruction—necessary, really, throughout the corporation—on how to work for somebody. The content of courses offered new supervisors is, logically enough, how to supervise. "How to work for somebody" is even more significant and necessary as a course. Most training courses in how to supervise are ineffective because the persons taking them have not first learned how to work for somebody.

Performance training should move on to a still more fundamental aspect. After meeting the person's needs to cope with those superior in power and the organization's needs to show people how to work for somebody, training should show people how to analyze their own performances. For example, in most organizations the annual reports we have asked managers to prepare have been confused, lacking causal relationships between what the managers did and operating results of clear benefit to the company, and therefore unconvincing.

The final feature of training the performer should be instruction on how to get persons in power to understand the possibilities of the performer's job—how to gain support and understanding of career potentialities from superiors.

Training the Appraiser

Attribution research has shown that people performing tasks concentrate on what they are trying to do; observers tend to see the personal or style characteristics of the performers. Thus appraisers see things that performers do not. That is part of their value and, in any event, is their nature. On the micromap, this means that areas observed by the performer are different from those observed by the appraiser. The performer sees what he or she is trying to do, and the boss sees more "distal" qualities. In terms of training, this means that we train the performer to work with data from Areas 7 and 8, but the appraiser has additional areas, especially Areas 1 through 6.

This distinction leads to a difference in focus, but it does not mean that appraisers need no help in such distinctions as between action and result. Supervisors often confuse effort with excellence, and performers (who want primarily to be judged for what is controllable, which is Area 7) can persuade an easygoing supervisor that results are less important than effort. This is, however, like saying that the company had a profitable year because it spent a lot of money. Area 7 represents inputs of energy, time, and money. Area 8 alone can show outputs. Appraisers need instruction in obtaining data for Areas 7 and 8 as well as the differences between them.

However, it is better to speak of *negotiating* the performance account than merely of obtaining data. Because there are conflicts of interest in all performance appraisal, negotiation as in labor relations is better than the PA-1 concept of the performance interview. PA-2 requires training in negotiating with the performer to develop a complete account of what has happened, to work out a plausible explanation of that account, and, on that basis, to formulate a set of expectations for the future. The goal of this negotiation is productivity rather than conflict reduction. Hence, if the two parties do not reach consensus on what has happened and why, the appraiser should offer an assumption and proceed to the next phase of the negotiation. In that sense, appraisal is closer to hiring than it is to labor relations.

The Appraiser as Performer

Appraiser training must follow performer training. That is, the direction of the PA-2 program is from the top down. First, we ask the president of the corporation or the general manager of a division to rethink the process by which he or she accounts to the board. This analysis lays the basis for appraising the persons next in command. They, in turn, must become as clear as possible on how they are accountable (the president helps them do this). Only when they are clear as to the method and content of their accountability are they equipped to appraise their subordinates. In this way, the installation of a PA-2 system moves as far down a corporation or a division as it continues to repay the effort.

The Appraiser versus the Performer

There is always a conflict of role and of interest between appraisers and performers. First, to observe performance is not the same as performing—thus, the role difference. The better one's performance, the less one is qualified to observe it: if one thinks like a golf coach when making a swing, the swing cannot be good. Second, a conflict of interest appears whenever two persons are in an authoritarian relation in which the superior is credited or blamed for the performance of the subordinate. This natural conflict tends to divide the two parties on both success and failure, the boss accepting success as his or her own and attributing failure to the subordinate, and vice versa. While these conflicts of role and interest may be regarded in a low-key manner and are accepted humorously, especially by mature executives, PA-2 assumes that they are nonetheless intrinsic. This fact leads us to treat negotiation as the essential characteristic of the communication taking place in PA-2.

Common Ground

The common ground of the two parties lies in evidence. It is in the long-term interest of both to perceive reality: evidence of performance. In the early phases of negotiation, both parties seek to build an agreed body of evidence of what happened. The more substantial and verifiable this body of evidence, the better the negotiation will resist the divisive forces outlined above. Evidence is a logical concept. It implies verifiable facts or plausible accounts of what happened, given in enough detail to link the key outcomes with a narrative account of events leading to those outcomes. Often the events will produce the outcomes in a cause-and-effect fashion, but not always. Managers must often be satisfied with plausible conjecture.

Causal Analysis and Attribution

Attribution research studies the way people attribute causes to one another's behavior. A football coach who observes a missed block has several options; if he attributes the block to indifference, the player is in trouble. The coach may pass the missed block off as an accident, or he may run a film and search for errors in the movements of the player which caused him to miss the block. These steps lead to different attribution searches. We are interested primarily in the attribution search called "causal analysis." A coach who chooses this method can help motivated players; similarly, causal analysis is the way managers help employees who are motivated. But what kind of analysis is appropriate when employees are not well motivated? Rather than blowing his stack if a player looks indifferent, the coach can make a causal analysis of the lack of motivation. While motivation causes action, it in turn is caused by other events. Since the manager can investigate these events, causal analysis is always possible unless the performance is accidental. Causal analysis requires evidence, and managers using PA-2 therefore must learn the meaning of evidence of performance and the related processes shown in the micromap. These are the proper topics to be treated when we train appraisers.

CONTRASTS BETWEEN PA-1 AND PA-2

Many seasoned readers will see points of common sense in the preceding analysis and say, "I can buy this idea. In fact, that is

TABLE

2–1

CONTRASTS BETWEEN SYSTEMS

PA-1 characteristics

1. Is designed originally to produce objective ratings of production workers.

2. Seeks multiple benefits.

3. Assumes a good climate and willing supervisors.

4. Covers all jobs, especially at lower echelons.

5. Emphasizes training the supervisor to review performance.

6. Completes rating form as the primary document, that is, a report card.

7. Files data which become liabilities under equal-opportunity laws and are almost useless for purposes of validation.

8. Depends primarily on two forms of feedback: knowledge of how one is doing and rewards for good performance.

9. Assumes conflict is preventable by good human relations; the two parties ideally should agree on ratings made.

10. Presents reducing authority differences (as in participative management) as one way to reduce conflict.

what I already do." However, PA-2 is not the rule in most companies despite occasional points at which their practice may be in agreement with our design. For one thing, the personnel department usually has designed 98 percent of the system, and the line 2 percent. How can this imbalance be? Professional personnel people want a line-managed system of PA, and yet they get stuck with the job. In PA-2 the chief designer of the system becomes the operating head of the division. How else can it be, since PA (at least PA-2) is *the company's structure in action?* It is delegation, chain of command, and all the other principles of organization as they actually work.

1. Transmits the influence of general managers, especially of the president.

2. Seeks one central benefit.

3. Does not require an ideal climate or cooperative supervisors.

4. Covers only jobs which have defined results.

5. Emphasizes training everyone to work *for* somebody.

6. Prefers a blank page over a rating form.

7. Files verifiable working accounts—whose most important feature is their value as evidence.

8. Depends on many forms of feedback (see micromap), since many more than two forms are operating.

9. Assumes conflict is intrinsic to the situation; the common ground is building a causal picture of what has happened, not ratings.

10. Views authority as less important than the intrinsic gap between any observer and any performer.

There are many points at which PA-1 differs from PA-2; some have been mentioned, and others are consequences of what we have said. These are presented in Table 2-1.

Some readers will see similarities between MBO and PA-2. As mentioned earlier in this chapter, this is a plausible observation, and we agree with it. But it ignores key features of PA-2 such as causal analysis. Management by objectives, as usually presented in published literature, seems to concentrate on Area 8. It is true that a solid MBO program probably goes on to the other areas and necessary feedback links shown in the micromap, but in this case MBO is being made into PA-2, and the differences evaporate.

SPECIAL PROBLEMS OF PA-2

PA-2 appears to correct some irrelevancies of PA-1, but our experience with the new system shows points at which it poses new and interesting difficulties.

PA-1 May Be Working

Through the Herculean effort and high professionalism of the personnel department, PA-1 may well be working in a company that has a good climate and cooperative supervisors. If these supportive conditions disappear, however, the weakness of PA-1 will be speedily exposed. That would be a good time for the company to consider shifting to PA-2.

Jobs May Be Designed for PA-1

A professional personnel department may well have designed the company's jobs so that they lend themselves to appraisal under the old system. In that situation, the labor of redesigning the whole organization may well exceed the gain from PA-2. However, the next time that the company contemplates organizational restructure, it should design jobs so that they may be appraised under the PA-2 system.

Autocratic Top Management

A company may have at its head or at the top of its divisions managers who either think their influence is absolute (and thus do not need PA-2) or are of such an autocratic character that we dare not give them any more power. The first problem is more serious than the second; PA-2 gives executives greater control over performance results than over people. Thus PA-2 adds to an executive's reach in the organization, but in the narrow band of increased control over results and not in the broad band of control over attitudes, motivations, and people. As an example, the typical PA-1 form required supervisors to rate personal traits, and it was not uncommon to rate people on their conduct, appearance, and leadership—all psychological qualities. PA-2 abolishes this kind of rating as an invasion of privacy and an irrelevancy.

Jobs without Results

PA-2 begins by defining the results met or missed by a particular performer. This procedure focuses on real outcomes, visible to persons other than the performer. Such outcomes fall into a few specific classes:

- Economic survival of the organization, including sales, finance, and cost control
- Inducement of change and innovation
- Production of marketable services and products
- Maintenance of organizational cohesion, provided this cohesion is consistent with the other goals

The problem is that, with proliferation of so many new types of technology and staff services, many jobs do not directly produce such results. Performance in jobs of this type can be appraised only by assuming that the visible results are linked to one or more of the above basic classes. A good example is advertising. It is rarely easy to show how advertising influences sales. We have to assume that increasing the number of readers who remember a magazine slogan will increase sales. Another example is personnel work. But here, at least, the personnel department, by increasing resources (Areas 1 and 3) directly influences the performance process according to the micromap.

The Thought Required

Even after results have been defined and documented, PA-2 is not simple. To reconstruct the events leading to those results requires an effort to recall events which may not have been noticed, much less recorded or remembered. The energy required to carry out PA-2 can come from two main sources:

- The example of executives at the top who undergo the process themselves. This will influence those who identify with these executives.

- The intrinsic reward of undertaking an intellectually interesting and intriguing search for causes. Such an analysis is more like a detective's investigation than like filling out the report card used in PA-1.

Written Accounts

The task of reconstructing what happened and why it did is so intricate that it demands the use of written accounts. This is something most managers resist. Until fully explained, the accounts appear merely to add to the paper flood. Most Americans do not like to write, as Marshall McLuhan explains, and perhaps PA-2 runs counter to an overwhelming trend. People graduate from high school and college without being able to write clearly. However, the reasons for written accounts will become apparent as we move further into PA-2. In essence these reasons include the following:

- Written accounts make it possible to revise one's presentation on the basis of critical thought, while verbal accounts are discursive or linear; mere utterances cannot be evaluated later and revised.

- Written accounts are 180 degrees away from the checklists or boxes of the typical personnel form used in PA-1. They thus provide the substance to replace the rating.

- Written accounts are evidentiary, offering an essential legal defense of what has been filed.

Fallibility of Memory

In the PA-1 system managers simply do not remember (if they ever did observe) the bases for the things they are supposed to rate.

Embarrassed by this failure, some managers do not want to have a review at all; others provoke ill feeling by the arbitrariness of their evaluation. While the PA-2 system requires ability to reconstruct past events, this ability is inherent in the nature of management. There is a time gap between action and results, as in a manager's commitment to build a new plant. This gap separates the initial action and the economic results which will ultimately determine whether the decision was wise. Filling in this gap is necessary to manage at all, not just to conduct PA-2. In other words, if results cannot be related to actions, a manager can neither manage nor be appraised. We must solve this problem in management whether or not we favor a PA-2 system.

In research at the Glacier Metal Company, Elliott Jaques found that a good measure of the size of a person's responsibility was the time span, "the maximum length of time the decisions made by a person on his own initiative committed resources of the Company" (1972, p. 23). This time span, which is also the period which would elapse before someone normally thinks it necessary to review a performer's results, was correlated closely with expected earnings. Compensation level, level of work, and time span were found to be related. Applied to our analysis, this principle means that the time gap between action and results may well be what we compensate managers for.

Crisis Management

According to Henry Mintzberg's study (1973), most managers work in the present on an ad hoc, informal, and conversational basis. They do not manage in the way rational models and PA-2 seem to assume but are preoccupied with immediate pressures and crises and ignore long-term objectives. No true performance appraisal of managers would appear to be possible without extricating them from this preoccupation with the present, especially in the light of the gap between action and results. Crisis managers are always in action and do not "waste time" relating present results to past actions, which seems to them like crying over spilt milk.

AN ENTREPRENEUR AS A YOUNG MAN

Dan went to Dartmouth College as a national merit scholar in 1960. He did well enough in grades but felt that the scholarship was not large enough to keep him going. Later he wrote, "The summer before our junior year, a close friend and I decided to start a business on the campus and chose pizza as our best chance for success. We lined up a bank loan to cover the equipment (in Detroit before going back to school) and also found a source of supply for high-quality pre-made "shells," or crusts, and sauce. Armed with this information, we went to see the head of the university's food service operation, outlined our plan, and asked for permission to deliver on campus from a location in town. He thought the idea had a lot of merit and suggested a 50-50 partnership whereby the university would provide the facilities and equipment and we would provide the management. The business would be turned over to the university at graduation time. By that time, after two years, the business employed some thirty students on a part-time basis and two delivery trucks on a full-time basis. The profit was approaching $1000 a month. My partner was killed shortly after we started. Part of the profits went to an educational foundation set up in his memory."

The preference for this ad hoc style would not lead managers to prefer the PA-2 system, with its demand for longer-term perspectives and written documentation. The training advocated earlier in this chapter releases managers from their preoccupation with the present. Although PA-2 is thus a means of release, however, it is certainly true that fire fighters (crisis managers) would at least initially resist PA-2.

TYPES OF WORKING ACCOUNTS

The accounts which managers or others offer of their own performance are a mixture of self-justification and fact. We make no claim that people are totally objective in the PA-2 system. However, asking a person to offer his or her own version of how things have

LATER EVENT IN DAN'S CAREER

Dan went to work for the XYZ Corporation. Several years later, when he was vice president of marketing for one of its major divisions, a vocational training school, he encountered a problem of students' registering for a course but not showing up. This expensive attrition was due partly to overselling by the national sales manager's force. Dan wrote, "Finally I reached the inescapable conclusion that, despite protests to the contrary, there were basic policy differences between myself and the NSM. . . . I had to admit that I had been fooling myself about this manager for over a year. Second, I had no one really ready to promote. As a result, I had to take control temporarily of the sales force in order to implement the changes I felt were necessary."

gone and why provides at least a starting place for negotiation. The accompanying accounts (Cases 2–1, 2–2, and 2–3) are typical of those collected in more than twenty projects that surveyed the performance of managers and professionals. They range from brief accounts of specific accomplishments and failures (critical incidents) to annual reports and to the long-term accounts we call "track records."

Many accounts do not clearly state the objectives of the persons' work. Organizations differ in the extent to which managers' and employees' annual reports show an MBO orientation (Table 2–2). We find that most managers stumble in preparing accounts, but we also find that they can readily be helped to do a more coherent, persuasive, and fact-based job of preparation. Most of them agree fairly quickly that the critical incident is highly relevant to management, although the annual report is more controversial. The average manager knows that the corporate president must prepare such accounts, but the manager would rather not follow suit. We see no reason that the president should be more accountable than other people.

DAN'S FIRST MAJOR ENTERPRISE ON HIS OWN

After Dan Kelly received his degree from Dartmouth in 1964, he served in the marketing department at Motorola for 3 years, receiving three 25 percent raises. He then went on to graduate school in business, completing his M.B.A. at Michigan, where he was a fellow and on the dean's list. He concentrated on finance and accounting. Following the M.B.A., he started with the XYZ Corporation at $18,000 a year, rising to the position of vice president of marketing for his division and receiving five increases in 5 years averaging 12 percent per year. He was making $32,000 on leaving.

Dan Kelly left the XYZ Corporation to found a business school for liberal arts graduates. In his judgment, a school was needed to serve those who could not invest the 1 to 2 additional years required for the M.B.A. degree. The school was to offer a 3-month total-immersion postgraduate course emphasizing such subjects as accounting, financial analysis, and marketing. Eighteen months later the school was booming, with a student body of more than 120. The school was granted formal status as a candidate for accreditation by the North Central Association of Colleges—the first time such status was granted a for-profit institution.

TABLE
2–2

Performance Index   of Different Groups of Managers

| | Percentage | | |
Managers	Very low	Moderate	Very high
12 public utility	50	50	0
55 state agency	16	84	0
44 manufacturing	5	73	22

The performance index was a score assigned to the annual report. Two factors were scored: degree of favorability in results and verifiability of facts presented as evidence for the claimed results. A high index required both factors be high; in other words, the two factors were multiplied. If one factor was 0, the total score also was 0.

3

WORKING ACCOUNTS

Top managers must be top diagnosticians of their operations. PA-1 failed because it could not diagnose the causes of effective or ineffective performance. PA-2 will succeed if you use it diagnostically. How can you do this?

Some managers depend on quantitative data to stay in touch with their operations. This is essential, but it is not enough. Managers must also rely on the reports subordinates give them. In this chapter we will show how such reports, when given in a form we shall call "working accounts," will give a cause-and-effect picture of each individual's performance. To do this, you must be ready to ask for explicit reports that are organized to investigate, explore causes, and (perhaps this will not seem businesslike) give vent to feelings.

Working accounts require the collaboration of your people. People will be willing to engage in thorough investigation if you are obviously fascinated by the operation—by the investigative side of management. They will see you as part experimental scientist, part investigator, and part good listener as they report the operation through their own eyes. To the extent that this happens, you will create a climate in which everyone is oriented to getting in touch with, and keeping you in touch with, the reality of the operation. When this happens, there is no time for political games. Meetings

A PLAIN-LANGUAGE REPORT (If you know the business)

(A manager writing an account of a key decision in which he took a chance.) Coke was something I knew little about except that we sold it cheaply because it was the absolute squeal of the pig: what's left after we squeeze all the good stuff out. We sold through refiners, who supposedly lined up freight cars and controlled the customer. We had little storage capacity, and the refinery would ship any car it could lay its hands on. One day a call arrived saying that we had 100 cars in Indiana unordered, unwanted, and impossible to unload in the user's yard due to a strike. Added to this, we were blocking trucks and had 12 hours before the railroad would return. Cost was a problem; so was an ability to take in, and no other customer would take that quantity. One option: quickly lease ground along side tracks and dump the product. I didn't have the authority. . . .

have fewer arguments and more collaborative solving of the giant jigsaw puzzle that any business is.

The working accounts your people provide will enable you to size up the work of individuals, to point to missing data, and, in brief, to keep posted on the real world. What kind of report will do that? It may be a plain-language report (Case 3–1); one written frankly, even if it is self-serving (Case 3–2); or sometimes one briefly describing a problem of the business, as in the form we call "critical incident." For example, a typical incident began:

> Shortly after I took over the area, I realized that a direct account was taking advantage of the company regarding spark-plug claims. They were purchasing extremely well, and I didn't want to rock the boat, but . . . .

So far such data sound like reports you already get. While they may sound familiar, there are some major differences between working accounts, as defined here, and the routine business reports to which you are accustomed:

A SELF-SERVING REPORT? YES, BUT WELL WORTH HEARING

In late 1973 I took over as supervisor of the night shift after having been a machine operator. I was a college student, younger than the people who would work for me. Though the job seemed to be a nice step upward, my satisfaction was tempered by the fact that key managers didn't seem to take the second shift seriously and would therefore play down any accomplishments. . . . During this time, I worked hard to make the shift a viable thing. I introduced a sheet system which took out a lot of confusion in our collating department. I tried numerous personnel techniques to improve the morale of the workers (the night shift thinks it's forgotten). For instance, we had a monthly dinner to which all the people on the shift would bring home-cooked foods. . . .

1. We are collecting evidence—raw material—for judging people, not data about an operation alone. This means that we are collecting human accounts and not tabulating data.

2. We want to distinguish the word *account* from *accounting*. For that reason, we will use the term "working accounts."

3. A working account differs from a report in that its structures and content focus on the individual in a situation, job, or series of jobs.

4. A working account is a type of personal account, not a new business or personnel form.

Personal accounts are frank historical reconstructions of one or more events significant to the persons concerned. They are written or told. Either way, they are efforts to build self-esteem, reduce tension, or clarify experience. A *working* account has all these goals, plus those of clarifying a person's experience for the sake of improving or maintaining the business operation. People tell such stories constantly, so often that storytelling appears to be a universal human need. You debrief yourself at home after a difficult day, at the pub over a drink, or in a reunion with old friends.

SHOULDN'T THIS BE FRANKLY AIRED?

In 1965, while working on the marketing project, our entire group was being measured to stay on schedule. A lot of overtime was being worked, and tempers were frayed. My boss seemed more concerned with staying on schedule than with the quality of the work. My assignment was tax accounting. The system then in use was poor and was being handled on tabulating machines. My boss kept insisting I take the tab system and convert it. In exasperation one day I said I would be damned if I would take an ineffective system and convert it to a third-generation computer. . . . He suggested I had better meet the deadline or look for a new job.

The obvious problem is that such accounts are both emotional and functional. When we develop a formal system of reporting in a business, we try to eliminate the emotional in the belief that this makes the report more objective. This is a serious mistake. While objectivity is desirable, it can't be obtained at the expense of freedom to "tell it the way it is." People need to level with each other, to spill their guts. *Formal* reports wash emotion out and lose something in the process.

Case 3–3 is an account written by a manager to a department to which he wanted to be transferred. Had he been unable to make such a report, his performance (and his present boss's recommendations) would have made no sense.

Because of their characteristic bureaucratic language, reports prepared in bureaucratic terms are not working accounts:

- Using the impersonal "It appears that" (instead of "I think") or similar phrases eliminates the individual.

- Using dispassionate, low-keyed statements such as "We made a sale" (instead of "This is the most impressive sale of my career" or "Hell, we would have sold twice as much if we had promised an earlier delivery date") makes it difficult to evaluate the account because everything seems routine.

- Merely listing the procedures followed makes the performer a carbon copy of everyone else who uses these procedures.

The working account conveys individual style. It permits humor and is sometimes entertaining. The idea behind official reports—that to be official is to be dull—ruins communication by forcing emotion underground.

While working accounts are unlike accounting data and bureaucratic reports, they do require discipline. This discipline, which will become clear during this chapter and Chapters 4 and 5, grows out of the features of working accounts which make them of great interest to managers on such occasions as the following:

- At the time of the annual review (Case 3–4)
- When handling an important transition (Case 3–5)
- Soon after a new appointee has gotten his or her feet on the ground
- At the close of a project
- On return from an important trip
- Soon after a significant success or failure
- When a new boss wants to learn recent developments from subordinates
- When evaluating someone for promotion

But are these accounts objective? The word *objective* is usually not well defined but is used as if it were self-explanatory. However, most accounts contain at least several points which are independently verifiable. They mention dates, places, and witnesses. This is as much objectivity as such accounts present and probably as

A VERIFIABLE ACCOUNT

In 1971 I was customer service manager, sent to this store as a stepping-stone to the training program. The manager before me was not concerned with the needs of the company but just with those of his associates. I was able to reduce the unnecessary labor he had put into the store, while showing associates that a two-way street ran between their needs and the company's. By adopting a semi-cash-control program, we were able to reduce cashier shortage from 0.075 to 0.03 percent. For one period lasting about a week, we had the total number of bad checks down to zero, owing to constant communication, verbal, written, and personal, going out to collect money owed. . . .

much as many of them need. Some accounts do pose problems, however, and we will return to the issue of objectivity below.

Key Features

Working accounts are narrative histories covering a period during which something of managerial interest has happened. The period may be as brief as a few minutes or as long as many years. While the history is free-form (there is no specific outline), there are ground rules, which grow out of the key features of working accounts:

1. The content of working accounts is rich enough to show why events occur as well as to describe the events.

2. Their open-ended character permits unexpected findings.

3. To the extent that the accounts describe the real world, they put the receiver in closer touch with the operation.

4. Conversational accounts offer the receiver opportunities for training.

5. Some accounts are not controversial. If the giver is permitted

MANAGING A CRITICAL TRANSITION

In 1969 I was promoted from the Kerry Junction store to Roadway. The new store was in a southern location, and the people there had the reputation of not talking to strangers. On arrival, I found the associates very proud of their achievements, but the prior management had neglected to inform them that the store was losing money on a regular basis. I felt my greatest challenge was to tell the truth and still maintain the associates' feeling of pride. I called a meeting and showed them the profit and loss statements. We drew up short-range goals and objectives and a long-range plan for the store and its associates. I relocated to the area to become a part of the local scene. . . .

to say what is on his or her mind—how, for example, he or she achieved an outstanding success—the performance appraisal becomes a pleasant occasion and strengthens the bonds between members of the team. Unfortunately, some managers show interest only in problem reports from their subordinates.

6. Other working accounts deal with situations involving strong feelings and spark controversy.

The problem of objectivity arises in regard to the sixth feature. Accounts of this type offer several versions of what happened. Negotiation—exchanges of views, turning the event this way or that to see it in a new light, perhaps direct conflict—is required to develop a final version of what really occurred. Ground rules arising from the six features, especially the last, will be outlined in the following chapters.

TYPES OF WORKING ACCOUNTS

Including examples in Chapter 2, three kinds of accounts have thus far been presented. These have varied in time from very brief to very long spans. The briefest are *critical incidents*. The middle-span accounts are *annual reports,* although a project might also be reported in this form. The longest are *managerial track records,* long series of annual reports. The three types differ substantially from traditional performance-rating forms in the following respects:

- There are no forms. The reporter just starts out with a blank piece of paper.

- A manager is asked to describe his or her performance in a recent incident, during the last year, or during the last several years.

- Working accounts include feelings, attitudes, and values as well as facts, actions, and the objective characteristics of situations.

- The accounts tell a story; they are historical. Thus they resemble a conversation in a bar more closely than they do a report written on a personnel form.

Working accounts also differ from conventional business reports along lines already mentioned, but they convey much information about the reasons for important business outcomes.

Among the biases or threats to objectivity in working accounts are these:

- The accounts contain a mixture of objective results convincing to others and of subjective results more convincing to the performer.

- While they may describe the actions taken to achieve those results, these actions are somewhat underplayed. Managers wrongly take it for granted that others will know what they mean and leave many gaps in their accounts.

- Managers often understate the role of the environment or of other people in general in producing a success.

CRITICAL INCIDENTS

Case 3–6 is part of a critical incident. If it were expanded to include more details and these details were verified, it would constitute an

A TYPICAL THOUGH BRIEF CRITICAL INCIDENT

Three weeks before Christmas, 1974, my assistant was transferred. My new assistant did not have any formal training, and I was scheduled for a week's vacation after Christmas. That gave me three weeks to prepare him to take my spot. First I explained the basic priorities: a clean, neat, fully stocked store. I found he was able to detect problem areas. Then we reviewed the people who would be responsible for solutions. . . . After 3 weeks of pumping my style and operation into his head, I went on vacation. When I came back, I was extremely pleased at the condition, sales, and payroll of the store.

example of very effective performance. (Others might question whether this manager should have taken his vacation, but since we believe managers should be judged on pragmatic grounds, we consider his performance effective.)

A critical incident is a work sample described in enough detail to show how the result was obtained or occurred. The concept dates to a paper by John Flanagan (1954) showing that Delco-Remy foremen (who traditionally resisted performance ratings) were willing to make an effort to review performance by citing specific examples. The production foremen saw the critical incident as a realistic way to describe employee performance. Instead of rating a person for output, which tends to routinize performance reports, foremen often prefer to record unusual instances. (In practice, foremen and other first-echelon supervisors tend to look only for negative instances, but that is another problem.) A critical incident in John Flanagan's definition can be either effective or ineffective, and a balanced portrait of a person's performance should include both good and bad incidents.

Since Flanagan's paper appeared, more than 500 papers based on critical incidents have been published by the American Institute for Research alone (Fivars, 1971). In brief, the critical incident is a basic type of personnel or performance data and one that is extremely significant in making studies of jobs, compensation, promotion readiness, labor relations, and grievances. Almost every imaginable personnel issue is illuminated by collecting pertinent critical incidents. Even ambiguous problems have been clarified by critical-incident surveys. A number of years ago the American Psychological Association developed a handbook as a guide to ethical practices by psychologists. To build documentation so that the guide would have teeth and not consist merely of vague aspirations, a research team under Nicholas Hobbs collected specific incidents in which a moral issue was involved in the behavior of a psychologist toward a client or a patient. From analysis of hundreds of these incidents, certain recurring ethical issues were defined and became the basis for the handbook.

In similar fashion, we have used incidents to study a variety of problems including:

- The job of foreign service officer for the U.S. Department of State

- The job of urban social worker

- The work of R&D laboratory administrator (from a survey of twenty R&D firms)

- The job of foreman

- The job of supermarket manager

- The jobs of general and staff managers (of manufacturing and refining companies)

- The jobs of pharmaceutical sales representatives

What the critical incidents show is small-scale occurrences. A waitress spills coffee on a customer. A police officer rescues a cat. A fireman goes into a burning building to save a life. A manager avoids a strike through a brief act of diplomacy. An engineer detects a major structural defect in a bridge during a casual inspection. These one-liners are not critical incidents, but if expanded, they may be. Each is part of an episode which, while complex, may occur in a few moments and therefore can be described in the manner of a newspaper reporter:

- Who?

- What?

- Where?

- When?

- The situation

- The options and risks

- The person's response

- The outcome

A good critical incident is not written in this sequence, but the narration should include all these features. We have found it possible to teach people to write critical incidents about their own performance.

Sometimes we have been given critical incidents such as Case 3–7, which patently omits at least one key fact: how the dismissed personnel were treated and how they responded. We are skeptical about the account. Much can be learned if you insist on expanding such an incident.

Working accounts usually turn out to be interesting, especially if the person is released from the hang-ups about writing that we all have when we try to be grammatical. For example, candidates for foreman at an automobile company were able to write interesting and relevant critical incidents when encouraged to use a casual conversational style. Relatively uneducated urban human-service workers were able to provide fascinating critical incidents, once assured that we were not interested in their spelling or sentence construction.

Commonly, a worker has feelings about an episode that are significant enough to recount. Those feelings are definitely a part of the original occurrence and should be put into the critical incident (Case 3–8). This is the main point in which we differ from Flanagan, a behaviorist. We do not see how human performance can be described adequately without the emotions of the performer, at least for any performance which is not routine. If an account pro-

WHAT IS MISSING HERE?

About 1972 the company was in a difficult profit position. It was apparent we had to consolidate, and I was asked to merge the sales functions, set up a new organization, and dismiss six or seven people.

I was pleased to be selected but concerned about the impact on sales morale and enthusiasm, particularly the effect on orders, as well as about the loss of key individuals. Speed of implementation was critical. Immediate decisions were made with the group president on the choice of four regional managers out of the five available, the boundaries of the regions, and similar choices for about twelve districts; we made these decisions in 48 hours. A telephone interview program with key people was laid out, and within a week all personnel changes were made. These were followed by a session in which everyone was given a detailed account of the reasons for the changes and of how decisions had been reached. Although some disappointments were evident, we had no morale problems, and the organization was back on track with minimum interruption.

ANSWER: Most managers see the last sentence as maybe a naïve cover-up. It just isn't detailed enough to accept.

---

duces significant results or failure worth talking about, it will include the performer's emotions: blaming of others, resentment of the situation, or perhaps gratification with success. These emotions are part of the reality.

Who Prepares?

A critical incident may be collected from the performer or an observer, or both. If the incident is collected from the performer, different features in the action will be emphasized than if it is collected from an observer. It is not that the one provides an objective account and the other a subjective account. There is no particular reason why a driver giving a critical incident describing how his or her accident occurred can never be trusted to give an objective

EMOTIONS ARE PART OF BUSINESS REALITY

I began my new job June 1 of this year as regional manager. When I arrived, I was probably the individual most hated by managers in the region. They had been passed over, and an outsider had been brought in. No one would have a drink with me or invite me around. It was the icebox treatment.

---

account. True, we like several witnesses to corroborate significant incidents. To impose this as an ironclad rule, however, would limit us to a relatively small population of incidents in the work of a manager. Consider the simple arithmetic of supervision. A supervisor who has several persons reporting to him or her cannot know most of what they are doing. If the supervisor cannot rely on their accounts of what they are doing in any respect and can trust only what he or she (as the only trustworthy observer of performance) can observe, the supervisor would have to spend all the time watching. The supervisor has other things to do. He or she appears to have a choice of relying on others' self-serving accounts or on personal observations which are too limited. However, there is a *third* alternative.

We can see this alternative most fully in the work of police chiefs. Most of the time, patrol officers in cars are not under direct observation. In fact, this is one of the causes of abuses of authority. A chief of police must rely on citizens' complaints of such abuses. What happens when the citizens complain and an investigation shows their complaint to be more or less justified? Something that resembles a critical incident goes into the files. However, it would be unfair to include in the dossier of a police officer only critical incidents written by angry citizens. The judgment of a chief of police who is overly preoccupied with investigations of citizens' complaints will be badly distorted. We have therefore suggested to a number of police departments that they find a way to include in their personnel files critical incidents of police work which are positive. Police officers, for example, could propose positive incidents representative of their performance. This suggestion has surprised some police chiefs and outraged others. However, it may be the only way to produce a well-rounded account of the performance of a police department.

We should obtain accounts from the most constantly present observer—the performer. It is possible to detect and discount the bias inherent in them.

Still more important, a chief executive has the option to interrogate subordinates about the content of the critical incidents they write about their work. Such a cross-examination is open to any boss. The main line of defense of the system's objectivity, it is part of the negotiation of the account.

LENGTHENING THE TIME SPAN

The critical incident is part of the mass of experience that is brought into focus for a reason. James McIntyre (1976) compares the incident with longer-term accounts:

> As the telescopic lens allows us to zoom in on details we never see with the wide angle, so does the writing of "critical incidents" allow us to see specifics against the broad narrative.

Different things can be learned from the zoom lens than from the wide-angle lens. Brief time periods allow us to see cause and effect in a more convincing way (long time periods contain too many intervening events between an action and the result). These causes can be seen not only in human relationships but also in technical matters. The weakness of incidents is that they cannot show the overall and long-range productivity of the individual.

Examples of what is seen in incidents are sales (made or missed), accidents, labor grievances, communications (such as critically important conversations with contractors), meetings, and

A REPORT WITH TOO MANY HOLES IN IT

In 1969 I was the division office manager for the Tacoma division. I felt the method of presenting performance data for the division was very unclear. I asked the division manager if I could take a shot at improving it. I did, and he was so impressed with my work that he asked me to explain it at the next division managers' meeting, which we were about to host. The executive VP also was there. My method was seen as a major improvement by the group, and the executive VP adopted it for all divisions. This led to his decision to assign me (this year) to the newly created systems department—a major turning point in my career. The format is still being used.

decisions. A manager who has had a conspicuous success should debrief himself or herself in great detail. Thus the manager can understand why the success occurred and repeat the procedure on another occasion. To train managers, ask for more specifics; in Case 3-9 the manager should go into much greater detail to show specific reasons for the success of his approach.

What cannot be learned from a single incident is whether any of the causal relations occur frequently and are typical of the person involved. It is evident that we must have many incidents and use a time span for accounts which permits things that cannot appear in short range to be seen. These include undertaking projects, introducing new products, bringing about mergers, planning and conducting sales campaigns, and getting a losing plant turned around. The higher the position, the more important these longer time spans.

ANNUAL REPORTS

We give managers very few instructions on preparing or presenting annual reports beyond, "What did the company get for its support of your programs and its investment in you?" It is surprising how few managers have considered such a question.

Why does it matter that an individual can present his or her own annual report? Doesn't every boss already know what has been going on? First, we believe managers who cannot give an account of their contributions to a company and the problems encountered in doing so cannot be fully and properly accountable. This circumstance causes the immediate superior problems, including not only concealment of poor results but glossing over the faulty actions or conditions which will continue to produce them. Second, such managers may be performing well but, unable to advocate their own cause, may fail to be credited properly and lose out to more assertive but less qualified competitors. Third, many managers do not report *any* results, good or bad (this problem particularly concerns staff managers' reports). On interrogation, such managers sometimes explain that they are not in the kind of work which produces results. An example is in Case 3–10. This manager did not prepare an annual report: he prepared a job description. In terms of the micromap, he was thinking of Area 7 only. He believed that he had a sizable job because he supervised thirty people. He implied that if he had more authority, he would do a better job. He never said what a better job would be or that he was then doing a good job. His job was evidently buried so deeply in the bureaucratic apparatus that its purposes were lost. In spite of the opinion of some staff managers that they cannot produce results, the individual in Case 3–11 did so.

What features in the annual report as normally written escape the critical incident? The critical incident is especially effective in showing:

- Day-to-day human interaction which creates communication, cooperation, and conflict

- Feelings and short-term motivations

- Accidental, one-shot, and immediate causes

HARDLY A RESULTS-ORIENTED REPORT

In the year 1976, functioned as head interviewer in the Albany claims office. Directly supervised thirty subordinates. Concerned with initial and reopened claims taking; warranting benefit payments and check disbursements. Served as buffer between general public and the supervising manager. A major difficulty was in supervising adjudicators who were comparable in pay grade.

The annual report, in contrast, shows these features more fully:

- Strategies of the manager in applying long-term effort toward the results sought

- Environmental pressures of some duration and persistence which made the results difficult to obtain (Case 3–12)

- Effect of actions taken over a long period (Case 3–13)

- The bottom line of overall results—what the company and the manager have to show for a whole year's effort by him and investment by them (Case 3–13)

Annual reports have limitations, chief among them being that work may not break down into annual units. A project may have been completed in October, and the annual report written in December. In this case, the project report should have been written in October. It is artificial to make everything conform to the annual accounting cycle. Some efforts commence in one year and come to fruition many years later, as in the planting of trees for a lumber company. A new plant manager sometimes cannot be evaluated for 2 or 3 years, at least if given an operation which must be turned around. Annual reports also underestimate the extent to which a manager is solving his or her problems. It takes perhaps almost as long to change the characteristic *modus operandi* as to acquire it in

A GREAT LITTLE REPORT, EVEN IF BRIEF

1973 was a fun year for me. We entered the year with a small quality-control engineering force and a major new product to bring to life. QC took over the tape-system run-up responsibility, integrating the 10-hour-per-system task, and by mid-April we had absorbed the run-up time into the standard test hours, knocking the 10 hours into oblivion. . . .

the first place. To expect instant behavioral change in a manager 40 years old is as unrealistic as to expect someone to stop smoking or drinking on a sudden decision.

What are we to make of the occupational differences shown in the MBO index in Table 2–2? Are these true occupational differences, or do they arise from our use of this form? We did not intend the table as a piece of pure research, but in general we think that the annual report finding shown there does reflect occupational differences. However, are those occupational differences necessary? (See page 45.)

MANAGERIAL TRACK RECORDS

The longest possible time span covers an entire career. It includes critical incidents and annual reports, combined to provide the total picture of a person's career. Properly and fully written, a document covering a career shows a great deal about strengths and weaknesses and the kind of values the person has provided the organization. Because of their breadth, such "biographies" have also included features not usually put in critical incidents and annual reports. Among them are the following:

- More detailed personal data. The major moves a manager makes over a long period cannot really be understood without understanding his or her personal life.

A TOUGH SITUATION DESERVING FURTHER EXPLANATION

In 1972 I was reassigned from a familiar home district to a district some distance away made up of overlapping old towns and cities. The new metropolitan area had eight offices, four of which had newly assigned managers this calendar year. In addition to taking on a new area, I was to introduce a new program emphasis. Staff in local offices, who had been predominantly serving the disadvantaged, now had to change their approach to outgoing job developers. This change required persistent efforts to convert the staff to a new type of worker. . . .

- Long-term goals, which we have found vital in describing the careers of high-level managers, appear in career biographies. These goals are obscure in critical incidents and annual reports.

- Subtle problems that cause persistent failure emerge in narrative accounts of biographical scope.

In other words, managers' biographies show what they are trying to do with their lives and work, in contrast to the variable pressures and opportunities presented in the shorter-term documents. Of what use is this material? Almost any situation involving long-term planning, such as promotions, development, and personal counseling, requires a biographical foundation rather than a critical incident or an annual report. We note that managers' biographies were one of the important pieces of information collected in the AT&T assessment originally reported by Douglas Bray (1966). From biographies AT&T was able to forecast promotion rates. Such biographies offer a promising degree of validity in estimating future performance.

WHAT CAN BE LEARNED FROM SUCH DOCUMENTS?

Over a period of years, we have conducted surveys by using such documents in a variety of forms. Without attempting to report

CASE

3–13

OFTEN ONE ANNUAL REPORT IS NOT ENOUGH

1970 was a year to build, evaluate, cut, reorganize, train, monitor, and recut. I joined this company in late 1969 to cut and reshape quality control and retrain the operation. In 1970 we removed almost all QC supervisors and replaced them with working leadmen. This was a year to reduce the head count from more than eighty-five, with five supervisors, to sixty-seven, with two supervisors. QC installed an employee motivational system to improve work output (it did) and started a manufacturing feedback system (that did no good). We introduced a special tape system and concentrated on reducing test and check-out costs. By the end of the year the systems were going through in about 50 hours each. By June of this year, we had turned the division around and were in the black.

---

precise and neat experiments here, since that is not our purpose, we would like to tease from these data, which describe several hundred managers, recurring findings that appear to illustrate the potential value of working accounts.

An "action quality" is a way of operating that consistently gets a certain type of result. We're going to describe some action qualities that are best revealed in each of the three kinds of accounts.

HOW TO FIND ACTION QUALITIES

An action quality is a blend of skill and effort in a given environmental setting. For example, a surgeon may use a bedside manner to soothe a certain type of patient before surgery. Describing that bedside manner in specifics would help us understand the surgeon's action quality. *Evaluating* the action quality requires determining whether it actually has the intended result. Some patients may interpret a bedside manner as evasive and irrelevant. Whether that is true must be determined by direct observation of what happens when the surgeon uses the bedside manner.

The examples of critical incidents and other accounts in this chapter may be analyzed to determine action qualities in the following way. First, underline the result which was the point of the report, good or bad. Second, review the report to see what the performer did that produced or failed to produce results. The reader should also decipher factors other than performance that could have produced the results. Since action always occurs in a situation, the reader should next attempt to characterize the situation in terms of the pattern of environmental supports and difficulties confronting the performer. It is with those supports and against those obstacles that the individual always performs. Until we can determine how the situation looked to the performer, we cannot understand the options he or she sought. It is only from the options that appeared possible and reasonable to the performer that action could proceed.

ACTION QUALITIES OFTEN SEEN

The following track record qualities usually require a record of more than one year, on more than one job, in bad times as well as good, and for more than one boss:

1. Showing long-range leadership

2. Facilitating the economic survival of the organization

3. Inducing a sluggish bureaucracy to act

In addition, there are several action qualities which can be shown in annual reports and critical incidents as well as in track records:

4. Confronting difficult situations

5. Inducing growth and innovation in others

6. Providing quality products and services

7. Maintaining cohesion and order

8. Tenaciously pursuing goals

Certain action qualities are specific to annual reports:

9. Showing good judgment of people

10. Goal setting

Finally, action qualities specific to critical incidents include:

11. Reporting to someone

12. Engaging in applied quantitative analysis

13. Participating in communications transactions

14. Showing interpersonal flexibility

15. Fact-finding

ANALYSIS OF ACCOUNTS

Longer accounts demonstrate managerial value insofar as they show how a manager works toward such results as economic survival (Action Quality 2), innovation (AQ-5), production (AQ-6), and cohesion (AQ-7). While these are the criteria for managers, we don't list them first. Instead, the action qualities are shown in rough order of importance for two factors: level of responsibility (usually the delay between action and accountability, as explained earlier) and compensation paid. Below are suggestions for what to seek in appraising performance accounts for these qualities.

Action Quality 1: Long-Range Leadership

This quality refers to a manager's articulate and persuasive presentation of a desirable future. Visualize a president addressing his or her board and saying, "This is where we can go in 5 or 10 years." A future picture is painted not only in terms of a profitable status but in terms of product quality, position in the market, geographic location, or other factors which appeal to the board and which the president can *substantiate*. This is a realistic presentation that the president can defend and advocate with facts. We can visualize such a presentation being made by a political figure in attempting to get elected or by the president of a university in endeavoring to rebuild faculty morale. Our initial survey using critical incidents in published accounts of the careers of eminent managers led us to see long-range leadership as a key action quality. Our method was to study documents of managers who varied in reputation from the nationally eminent to the locally prominent. (We don't want to demean the manager who is known only locally. We are referring here to reputation, not to competence.) We found that managers who were known nationally tended to look ahead from 5 to 10 years. Local managers, whatever their good qualities, did not do so in the published incidents. Because we worked from published documents, these findings have obvious limitations. However, in a number of subsequent studies we have found this long-range perspective or long-range persuasiveness in other documents written by eminent managers. It is a necessary quality for a person who wishes to lead an organization somewhere new or somewhere difficult.

Does looking ahead mean anything? Is it possible? Glen Carlson and the senior author ran an experiment in which we found that some people can forecast events as specialists do. We called that experiment Project Delphi. We gave the subject an event, such as the year in which there would first be a live landing on Saturn, a colony on the moon, or other scientific event, or something nearer at hand, like facsimile newspaper printing in the home. We asked the subject to estimate the year by which that event would be plausible—the year when it would have a 50–50 chance of occurring for the first time. This method was used in the original Project Delphi developed by the Rand Corporation. What the Rand Corporation did was to run the Delphi experiment with population specialists, forecasting, for example, the year by which the world would have 8 billion people. What we found in duplicating this experiment was that average managers make assessments as specialists do. In short, it appears possible to measure future perspective quantitatively. This ability to visualize the future is part of Action Quality 1.

Action Quality 2: Economic Survival of the Organization

This quality refers to a manager's ability to influence the economic survival of an organization. It is a general management quality. Action Quality 2 refers to the economic output of the organization as influenced by the manager. It can be shown only by someone in a position of considerable authority and discretion. Like long-range leadership, it can be appraised only after a person has moved toward the top. In Table 3–1 we have listed all the action qualities and shown the earliest level in an individual's career at which the respective qualities can be perceived. Economic survival can usually be perceived only beyond middle management. It includes two factors. One consists of characteristic results such as profits, sales, cost control, and financial management. The other factor comprises activities contributing to those results. This factor is very difficult to appraise, because it is hard to know exactly what a particular executive did to achieve corporate profits. In practice, we can appraise the following:

1. In any given year, did the manager perform economic-survival functions as a major responsibility?

2. In that year, was his or her *influence* over those functions a major one?

3. What was the economic effect of that influence?

The first two questions can be answered with some objectivity. The third requires a committee in a position to make an appraisal. Hence most research on Action Quality 2 will be based on functions and influence.

Is the broad economic-survival action quality limited to business firms? It would seem possible to appraise it also in voluntary-sector organizations, since the quality includes fund raising, cost control, and financial management. In government organizations, it would include legislative relations that affect the budget, cost control, and financial management. There seems to be no clear reason why economic survival is any less required of top manage-

TABLE
3–1

POINT IN CAREER AT WHICH AN ACTION QUALITY CAN BE CONVINCINGLY DOCUMENTED*

	Career stage		
Action quality	Initial		Advanced
1. Long-range leadership	X X X	X X X	X X
2. Economic survival	X X X	X X	
3. Sluggish bureaucracy	X X X	X X	
4. Confronting difficulty	X X X	X	
5. Inducing innovation	X X X	X	
6. Production	X X X		
7. Cohesion	X X X		
8. Tenacity	X X X		
9. Judgment	X X X		
10. Goal setting	X X X		
11. Reporting	X X		
12. Quantitative analysis	X X		
13. Communications	X X		
14. Interpersonal flexibility	X		
15. Fact-finding	X		

*X means that the action quality cannot yet be easily detected. For example, long-range leadership cannot be readily detected until a sufficient number of years have passed.

ment in government and voluntary-sector organizations than it is in business. In our research with managers from a number of business organizations including electronic, automobile, grocery, and oil companies, we have found that this factor is related roughly to compensation. We do not know whether it is similarly related in public or voluntary-sector organizations.

Action Quality 3: Inducing a Sluggish Bureaucracy to Act

This quality refers to intervention with or without authority in a situation in which the status quo is self-defeating, that is, a situation in which someone maintains a policy or procedure even though it is costing the organization its economic shirt. A manager with this quality normally has a strong power drive but is harnessing it in the service of achievement for the organization. In other words, he or she is strongly motivated to break the circular chain in which policies are being enforced for no apparent reason other than self-perpetuation in power.

Particular difficulties are involved in appraising this action quality, which is shown briefly and sometimes dramatically in a manager's history. That is, he or she interferes with the status quo. For this reason, intervention is often followed by political flap or even by a bad performance rating. (This is one of the many reasons why managerial appraisal has little to do with performance ratings as defined in textbooks.) However, this interfering behavior, if persistently shown in many situations, suggests something else. Action Quality 3 is functional, often limited in duration, and directed against a self-defeating status quo; it is not professional radicalism. It is extremely important to appraise this action quality very precisely. The quality must be appraised in a carefully reconstructed and verified performance history. For an exemplary project illustrating how this action quality can be perceived, we cite our study of medical sales representatives for a pharmaceutical house. We learned in a detailed study of the sales records of these representatives that a major factor in determining who was going to get sales and who wasn't was willingness to interfere with a sluggish and bureaucratic health system.

Action Quality 4: Confronting Difficult Situations

An individual showing this action quality seeks difficult situations, as seen in his or her critical incidents, annual reports, and longer-term documents. These may be selling situations, in which the difficulty consists of inaccessible or resistive customers. In appraising Action Quality 4, we must take care to ensure that the individual is not merely inflating a situation to explain poor performance:

"What could anyone do? It was an impossible situation." In the project which best exemplifies this action quality, we found that pharmaceutical sales representatives progressing most rapidly were systematically tackling harder and harder situations in contrast to representatives whose careers appeared not to be progressing. In considering this action quality, we need not attempt to determine whether the person concerned is succeeding. Normally people do not tackle hard situations unless they have succeeded with easier ones. In spite of the subjectivity of the concept, it is not hard to get seasoned observers of a particular job to agree on which situations are more difficult and which are less difficult. We can thus track the progress of people in setting higher goals for themselves much as we track the progress of a high jumper who keeps moving the bar higher.

Action Quality 5: Inducing Growth and Innovation in Others

Unlike Action Quality 3, this quality concerns the objective output of a person's influence over others. His or her action causes growth and change in others' ideas or productivity. Creative engineers show this action quality. Dynamic managers show it. Good trainers show it. Such managers are consistently cited by subordinates as contributing to their growth; obtain patents or copyrights of economic and scientific value; have subordinates, associates, or bosses who move to better assignments in a way traceable to the performance contributions to their work; or strike creative sparks at meetings—either operating meetings, training sessions, or bull sessions. The motivation involved in this action quality is taking an interest in the progress and growth of others. Managers of this type usually need not be coached to conduct performance reviews or provide developmental counseling. In R&D settings, however, this action quality may not take the form of such formal, helpful interaction; rather, it appears in research conferences or in formal idea sessions in which there is a vigorous interchange of scientific ideas. We questioned the managers of twenty R&D firms about incidents in which they showed effective or ineffective interaction. We found an essential ingredient in the R&D setting to be the mediation of conflict: the successful R&D administrator fostered innovation by the way in which he managed conflict. Indeed, innovation often seems to come out of the clash of ideas. Can we measure this action quality in the laboratory? There has been a great deal of research in measuring creativity, but so far it seems tangential to Action Quality 5.

Action Quality 6: Providing Quality Products and Services

This quality is characteristic of a manager who gets something done, specifically something that produces a tangible result of value to others. Like Action Qualities 2 and 5, this production must have a tangible result: a socially valued product or service. A manager must show this action quality if he or she is going to produce income and social justification for the company's existence. In manufacturing, for example, that means making a product which meets quality standards and proves salable. In medicine, it means health care which meets patients' needs. It should be obvious that a performance rating does not prove that an employee is producing a service or product of value to others if the rating means only that the boss thinks well of him or her. However, when in a position to assess the product or service produced by the employee, the boss should rate that product or service. In other words, the output is rated, not the manager.

Action Quality 7: Maintaining Cohesion and Order

This quality is the *corporate* dynamic; that is, it unites, whereas the innovative action quality pulls things and people apart to resynthesize them into something creative. Therefore this action quality is often in conflict with Action Quality 5, and when it is, the manager must learn to mediate. Action Quality 7 is thus complex. In the first instance, the manager is responsible for maintaining orderly standards and policy-conforming performance; if something such as a creative innovation happens, the integrative manager is responsible for bringing the corporation together in a new accommodation which includes the innovation and yet maintains cohesive order under the new arrangement. A manager who can *maintain* cohesion only until there is disruption has less of this action quality than a manager who can *restore* cohesion. Both aspects belong to the action quality, however, and help define it. This action quality usually is shown in the development of good human relations, their consolidation and communication, and the use of well-understood standardized procedures. To some extent the corporation must stay in step. In brief, Action Quality 7 is required of staff managers in all fields: accounting, personnel, data processing, information services. Any manager who assists others to function and provides data to aid them is helping to maintain the cohesion and order of the corporation. The best example of a staff manager who functions at the higher level and restores cohesion after a creative disruption would be the labor negotiator or someone assigned to settle grievances.

Action Quality 8: Tenaciously Pursuing Goals

This is essentially an action quality of persistence. It can include an antisocial element, in that at times a manager must ignore feedback received from some other people. Such a manager appears a bit dense, seemingly ignoring what others are saying if it does not match his or her inner drumbeat. This appearance is deceptive, for the manager who excels in this action quality is merely selective about the persons from whom he or she will accept feedback. Feedback from an inferior or ill-qualified boss or peer will be ignored, while the manager will respond to the feedback of outstanding or creative peers or subordinates. For example, in our study of eminent managers, we found that they persistently ignored discouragement and disparaging comments by those whose long-term vision did not match their own.

Action Quality 9: Showing Good Judgment of People

This quality calls for a practical analysis of the people on whom one's performance depends most fully. They may be subordinates, superiors, peers, or customers. We have made rather extensive surveys of Action Quality 9. Thus far they support the assumption of a general judging skill (Dailey, 1971). We have measured two kinds of judgment, pragmatic and conventional. Pragmatic judgment is shown when a manager's decisions have expected consequences. Such a manager has "predictive validity." The second form of judgment requires conventional wisdom. Such a manager shows good judgment by drawing conclusions which are plausible to others who have reviewed the same evidence. Pragmatic judgment is more rigorous than conventional judgment, but some decisions must be made without the hope of obtaining criteria to verify their pragmatic wisdom.

Action Quality 10: Goal Setting

The setting of attainable and relevant goals is rather visible in annual reports. We do not consider that a manager should be credited for MBO unless he not only shows the ability to project and pursue goals but can relate actions and situations encountered to those goals. As in the judgment of people, the goals can be evaluated against both conventional and pragmatic criteria.

Action Quality 11: Reporting

This action quality is shown by a person accountable for his or her work. This means that the person must provide an account to *someone*. Learning to work for someone is a neglected area of management training; there is little in textbooks about it. Most managers are quite concerned about the persons or groups in power over them, but they receive little or no help in learning to report to those persons or groups, to influence them, or to negotiate with them. We developed an accounting-for-performance procedure in which the manager learned to present a persuasive but factual account of what he or she had done for the company in a given time period. At one company, for example, managers reviewed their own performance quite extensively and then made a video-tape self-presentation to be viewed by upper-management committees. In a government-agency client of ours, candidates for promotion did this in writing.

Action Quality 12: Engaging in Applied Quantitative Analysis

This quality involves having a good head for figures if one is in general management. The requirement of being able to *apply* mathematics to work settings makes us think that Action Quality 12 cannot be manifested convincingly by a person much below the middle-management level. While it is not difficult to find academic formal testing or even case methods of measuring applied quantitative-analysis skills, application is the important factor. That is, this is a quality of action, not of knowledge.

Action Quality 13: Participating in Communications Transactions

Transactions analysts work with specific dialogues which are a special type of critical incident. In such dialogues it is possible to determine whether a person's communications skills result from ability to reach another person as an adult, child, or authority. In dialogues showing communications "static," it is possible to determine whether the difficulty comes from crossed lines or, in extreme cases, from communications games resulting in a breakdown (Bradford and Guberman, 1978).

Action Quality 14: Showing Interpersonal Flexibility

This action quality is the equivalent of "contingency management." That is, good interpersonal relations to some extent depend on the particular situation. Instead of evaluating managers on whether they generally adopt a recommended technique of inter-personal relations, we can determine whether they use a full range, or repertoire, of techniques by evaluating them for this action quality. Proper choice from the range depends on the situation. The range of techniques is most easily illustrated by the four forms of influence style defined in the management-training program of Berlew and Harrison (1976): using reward or sanction, using as-sertive persuasion, appealing to common vision, and building trust. The first two of these styles are fairly assertive; the second two, more diplomatic. The influence styles are appraised through questionnaires devised by Berlew and Harrison and used by LeRoy Malouf (1977) at Polaroid, Rank-Zerox, Digital Equipment, and other corporations. Managers tend to be fascinated with their scores on these influence-style measures. They provide, along with the exercises used in Berlew and Harrison's management-training program, a set of laboratory measures of interpersonal flexibility.

Action Quality 15: Fact-Finding

This action quality is the mark of a manager who can collect perti-nent data and organize them in the form of a case. One important application is in interviewing new employees. Among other appli-cations are grievance investigations, sales reports, and perform-ance-appraisal interviews. Action Quality 15 requires not just in-terviewing skill but the particular skill of obtaining evidence which can be used to make good judgments. In a project for Pepsi-Cola we found that sales managers could be shown in a fairly short time how to use the fact-finding interview we call the track record inter-view. That procedure is described in Chapter 7.

THE STRUCTURE OF MANAGERIAL CAREERS

The action qualities are listed in Table 3–1 in the order of time span, but only roughly so. Long-range leadership, which by definition has the longest time span, is listed first. While there are features of economic survival (such as zeal in controlling costs and making sales) which can be observed over short time spans, managers receive scope for this action quality over time spans of a year or more. From this point down, the qualities would seem to be capable of documentation over briefer spans. This generalization represents only an average, since there may be very long documents which display Action Quality 15, fact-finding, and as we have said previously Action Quality 2 can be perceived over brief spans.

What difference does this ordering of action qualities make? First, if the time spans are long because there tend to be long gaps between an action and the results which will prove that action to have been well taken, there are important consequences. The primary, lower-numbered AQs would be characteristic of higher-level jobs and would be better compensated. Second, it would be easier to learn the higher-numbered AQs because the delay in feedback is shorter. Thus the primary AQs would be rarer, and perhaps it does make sense to compensate them better.

The ordering also shows where faster learning would occur among the young, who are more likely to enter the lower-level jobs in which they can acquire the highest-numbered AQs.

Finally, the scheme suggests which AQs can be measured. It is possible to devise a psychological test of any ability which can be simulated in a few minutes or hours and to devise an assessment-center exercise of any AQ which can be observed in as short a period as an hour or so. But certain AQs, for which the time of observation is long, can never be measured through simulation. Unfortunately, these are the ones which pay the most and are the most weighty according to our scheme.

Why not confine assessment to what can be simulated through tests and assessment centers? Does this seem fair? A manager complained that he had had many years of successful operation of his plant but blew that track record in a single 3-day period at an assessment center. This hardly seems fair.

WHY NOT JUST MEASURE OUTPUTS?

Some managers feel that they should be measured only by their objective outputs. In Action Qualities 2, 5, 6, or 7 the entire action quality is related to very specific and quantifiable outputs. Sometimes these outputs are not easy to appraise, but at least there is common agreement that these action qualities are necessary to run an organization. The difficulties in limiting action qualities to these four are:

- The four AQs are too current; in particular, they neglect the long-term development of a business, as in Action Quality 1.

- They are not sufficiently analytical. An output may be produced for the wrong reasons. An individual may succeed in making money this year (be successful in Action Quality 2) while failing to confront progressively more difficult situations as in Action Quality 4. This means that the individual is performing well objectively but is not exploiting all existing opportunities. The purpose of analytical assessment of performance is to show a manager what more can be done and not confine ourselves to documenting what is done. Sometimes a manager should be given credit despite failure to achieve output if other action qualities show managerial talent of such a high order that, given a normal year and support from others, we can expect good objective results from his or her work.

THE ENVIRONMENT

The foregoing attention to action qualities has neglected the entire reverse side of the coin. According to the formula assumed in the micromap, performance depends on three factors: motivation, skill, and environment. The action qualities are defined mostly in terms of the first two. What about the third factor as an explanation of performance results? The working environment deserves analysis in its own right, including:

- What kinds of situation exist when managers are getting their best results?

- What kinds exist when managers are getting their worst results?

The former analysis shows positive field forces, or "supports," for performance. The latter shows negative field forces, or "hindrances." A manager's history consists of supports and hindrances as well as action qualities. When we find a history which seems to show persisting support (let's say the manager always has a good boss), it may point to an additional quality of the manager. Why does he or she always receive support? Is it just luck? If there is a persisting hindrance from a boss, is the manager unlucky, or does he or she somehow cause this situation? These two examples of environmental analysis open the door to the exploration of two intriguing topics which unfortunately are outside our scope:

- Talent, or how to arrange a fast-track career
- Vicious circles, or patterns of unwitting self-defeat

ACTION SUGGESTIONS

Here are seven ways a key manager can get people to submit honest, complete, and timely working accounts, not just conversation.

- *Get balance into the accounts.* Show as much interest in what went *well* as in what went badly. You will build up among others the belief that you want to know what is going on, not just to nail them for what is going badly.

- *Make accounts human.* Where did the idea come from that being businesslike is being always cool and never emotional? You *know* that is false. When a subordinate or a boss is telling you about an important success or failure, he or she will drop clues as to his or her feelings. Come back to those clues in conversation. Say things like "That must have felt great" or "That happened to me once." If the other person really wants to unload, he or she will pick up your hint that you don't think it's bad to have those feelings.

- *Train top reporters.* Top investigative reporters come back with a story full of specifics. Nothing else holds water. Draw up a checklist, as in the subsection "Critical Incidents" above, when written or spoken reports come to you and use it to see what features are missing. When you apply this list enough times, others will get the message that you expect a complete report.

- *Focus on results.* It is human nature to talk about nonresults: our goals, our efforts, and the obstacles facing us. What you need as a manager is much more accounting for results. One way to get working accounts of this kind is to return reports when they consist mostly of nonresults. Say, "Rewrite this so that you start with the results I asked for, and tell me what worked to get those results or did not."

- *Ask for continuity.* Working accounts focus on the particular. Ask the reporter to tie the report to last year's and other people's reports. It will then be easier for you and for the reporter to see the big picture.

- *Make people account for their results.* Operating results, no matter how good or how bad, do not speak for themselves. Require an explanation of every result. When business is going well, the tendency is to think that no explanation is necessary. In fact, success is the most valuable thing in the world to explain.

- *Correct the antienvironmental bias.* When things are going well, managers are willing to point to their correct decisions and actions. When things are going badly, they point to business conditions and the "environment." Ask for the role of business conditions and the environment in *all* reports.

4

NUMBER MAGIC

The aim of this chapter is to get you to use numbers for what they do best in the analysis of performance. We shall find that numbers are overused and carry a burden of analysis that should be properly carried by words. Further, a pseudoscientific mystique is assigned to numbers, thus concealing abuses.

What numbers do best is to quantify certain limited, tangible, but important features of performance. Numbers do not create knowledge. They are applied to performance by people. A number applied to performance—for example, a performance rating—must be subjected to "cross-examination." Cross-examination means to trace the number to what it stands for: something observed, not a feeling. People quantify feeling when they rate a person as to how well they like that person, how favorably they regard him or her, or how promotable he or she seems. All these are improper functions of numbers.

What numbers *can* do is to contribute to the analysis of causes. To ensure this, we shall explain what we call "organic inquiry." An organic inquiry is an orderly process of reasoning about causes or results and possibilities of improvement. Numbers must not hide the language; that is, it must be possible not only to quantify but to discuss and clarify what happened, especially in context.

TABLE

4-1

PERSONNEL RATING FORM*

Instructions: Rate the incumbent on the following characteristics. Then explain any extreme ratings (far-right or far-left columns) below under "Comments." Indicate your rating on each characteristic by checking the appropriate line in one of the five columns.

	Far below minimum	Requires improvement	Average rating	Above-average rating	Far above average
1. Quantity of work output	___	___	___	___	___
2. Quality of work output	___	___	___	___	___
3. Initiative	___	___	___	___	___
4. Ingenuity	___	___	___	___	___
5. Persistence	___	___	___	___	___
6. Leadership	___	___	___	___	___
7. Reliability	___	___	___	___	___
8. Delegation	___	___	___	___	___
9. Follow-through	___	___	___	___	___
10. Adherence to policy	___	___	___	___	___

Comments:

*Adapted and abbreviated from a federal personnel form in use in 1977.

A Flagrant Example

A personnel rating form at a governmental agency (Table 4–1) merits comment:

1. The first two items are legitimate although vague.

2. Several other items might be legitimate, but only if rated in relation to the first two and not independently of them.

3. Most items involve an illegitimate use of numbers. They are "distal" qualities (inferential qualities, not directly observed) and should not be rated at all.

Later in this chapter we'll explain our views as to why these items are classified in this way and what can be done to remedy the situation. Here, we'll note only that the scientific invalidity, the economic uselessness, and, ultimately, the legal liability from an equal-opportunity standpoint are all due to the illegitimacies in this form.

QUANTIFY ONLY THE ESSENTIALS

The essentials of performance which should be quantified are those necessary to carry out an orderly process of reasoning, beginning with end results which are the purpose of the job and reasoning through to causes. To understand this principle, consider the micromap. In Figure 4–1 the key area in which to begin an organic inquiry is shaded. Then work back into the adjacent and immediately preceding area, which consists of actions in a situation. Only three things—results, actions, and situations—should be quantified (everything else is of a distal quality). If you do not know the results of a person's work, there are several implications. The first is that you are not prepared to rate performance at all. The second is that the job is improperly organized and perhaps even unnecessary, since it does not generate any visible or knowable results. If there are no knowable results, why does anyone consider the work useful or worth doing?

Figure
4-1

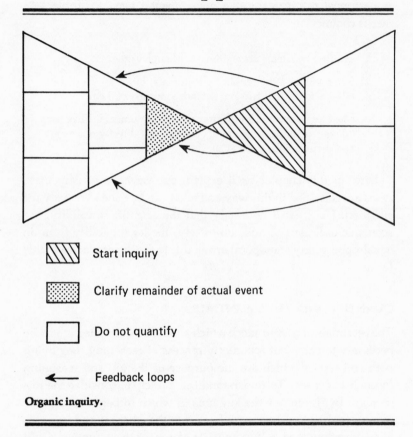

Start inquiry

Clarify remainder of actual event

Do not quantify

← Feedback loops

Organic inquiry.

EVALUATING RESULTS

We recognize four types of results or outputs in a business operation. If what you've observed cannot fit into any of these categories, keep looking until you can identify a ratable result. In any
productive organization, results are outputs which either serve client needs or help other people to serve client needs. The results or

LEGITIMATE NUMBERS: PROFIT AND OTHER RESULTS

As manager of quality assurance, I had many conflicting problems this year. We introduced a new system, QC bought a computer to perform system testing, and we achieved our goal in the core plant. The core plant was making 7 million servite cores per week with 35 percent yield. Increased sales required an increase to 100 million per week, so I claimed I could increase the yield to 70 percent in 3 months' effort. I analyzed the problem, moved to the core plant, installed a computer terminal in my office, and personally tested cores, mixed powder, learned the business, and put the whole thing on the computer. All control operators were transferred to QC. I hired a QC manager for the plant, cooperated with the plant manager in increasing capacity, and by late 1969 we were there—100 million per week at 70 to 85 percent yield. This year I also controlled the entire division capital budget of $3 million, helping each manager to justify new equipment. For the second year in a row we beat all records of dollar shipments and profit.

outputs which facilitate results are of four kinds: economic, innovative, cohesive, and productive. There are various ways to test whether these criteria are met. Some criteria are self-evidently met (Case 4-1). The simplest test is, "Will someone pay for the service?" Whether anyone will pay for the service or not, someone other than the producer must make the decision, "Yes, this output is what we had in mind in setting up this job." This decision legitimates the output, but it must be made by someone other than the one who produced the service. Someone closer to the customer or ultimate client of the organization must say that this output is a part of the purpose of this job. Expressions of legitimacy include:

- "Yes, I will purchase this result from that producer."
- "I must have this result—I will make my own operation wait until I do get it."

- "I would prefer to have this result from this particular department than from some other department."

- "If I could not get this result, I would have to hire somebody from my own department to provide it."

In other words, the producer of the result cannot directly judge its value to someone else. This is the first thing that is wrong with self-rating a performance. Rating a performance is a proper function of a person's immediate superior, but not all immediate superiors can quantify results. If they cannot, someone who will be able to do it must be found.

In practice, we have asked the performer to include in the annual report specific results which went well or badly. Some jobs make it easy to offer a highly quantified set of results which other people can certify as valuable, whether for economic or other reasons (Cases 4–2 and 4–3). Holders of other jobs, especially if they are concerned with innovation (for example, growth of people or ideas) or cohesion (for example, maintenance of organization), are hard put to offer quantified results. They can, however, say what they have to show for a year's effort (Case 4–4), with at least an occasional numerical result.

The first two items in the rating form (Table 4–1) call for results to be evaluated, and we think that is a good beginning. But thereafter the form does not follow a sequence characteristic of organic inquiry. One must, for example, go on to inquire whether the successes claimed were properly creditable to the person being rated or whether any failures should be blamed on him or her. At an early point we must rule out an environmental explanation of the results. By "environment" we mean anything outside the person, including the action of others. Obviously a person should not be rated for things over which he or she has no control. We must also decide at an early point whether the result is in the "judging zone." That is, a person should be judged for a result only if the degree to which the environment determines the result is less than a certain amount. Another way to put this is as follows. Make an early judgment as

LEGITIMATE NUMBERS: MBO

Was expected to complete and implement a material-requirements planning system. This was completed on schedule and is now a fully operative system that is the foundation for a capacity planning system by the computer.

Merge Star Corporation's manufacturing facilities so as to minimize the cost and impact on production. Completed on schedule with little or no loss to production—a superb job.

Met shipment objectives for the available backlog. Achieved on the average 95 percent of all backlog objectives which were established at the start of each month. The past-due was at about 800,000 at any one time in the first quarter of 1973. By the end of the year it was down to approximately 300,000 with the addition of many new products and the addition of another company.

With the perpetual inventory system I eliminated the need for a yearly physical inventory. Completed 75 percent of my MBO.

to whether any amount of performance would have been successful (note Table 4–2 below). Thus, do not rate a person for a failure if no one could have succeeded. If, however, you think anyone could have succeeded, given a strong environmental support system, do not credit a success (in Case 4–5 only a manager familiar with the market can decide).

Personal Causation

If the result is within the judging zone, there are still several possible alternative degrees of rigor in our reasoning. Here certain items in the sample form in Table 4–1 are pertinent. For example, in Item 3 initiative seemingly is pertinent, and yet initiative is a qualifying word rather than a specific action, as is true of many items in this

TABLE
4–2

DEGREES OF ACCOUNTABILITY FOR RESULTS

Performer

1. Passive. Performer (P) has no accountability.

2. Reactive. P is accountable only for response.

3. Managerial. P is accountable for what P anticipated or could have anticipated.

4. Strict. P is accountable for everything that followed P's actions.

5. Primitive. P is accountable for everything that happened, whether a consequence of P's actions or not.

Environment

1. Total. Environment (E) is seen as all-powerful.

2. Strong. Definite causes, if identified, are held accountable.

3. Correlational. E is considered to be associated only with outcomes.

4. Weak. E is merely the passive scene or occasion for performance.

5. Void. E is ignored.

Examples:

P1. P is seen as a mere tool.

P2. P is a crisis manager.

P3. A manager meets or doesn't meet the objectives set (MBO).

P4. A manager launches a new product, but unseasonal bad weather kills the campaign. The manager is blamed for the product's failure.

P5. A company fires its chief executive whenever profit and loss goes into the red.

E1. "Business conditions" are uncritically blamed for the manager's own failures.

E2. The company economist makes a critical analysis.

E3. Competitive price fluctuations are considered part of the explanation of performance.

E4. The state of the market is not given much attention.

E5. Environment is ignored.

---

form. Instead of describing behavior in an evaluative way, as this form does, it is better to describe actions factually at this stage of rating and later to see how well they are connected with the end

LEGITIMATE NUMBERS: PRODUCTIVITY

1973 was a banner year. I started out with the additional responsibility of the sustaining engineering function. Its goal was to solve numerous design deficiencies in our products, which it did. In November 1973 I returned the group, a lot sharper, to engineering. The year saw the integration of the star line with its myth of "super quality" into our products and the smooth cross-training of test, technical, and inspection personnel without a hitch. 1973 saw the introduction of the high-speed card reader and the passing of a 400,000-card reliability test on the product. Productivity in all the measured work areas of quality control was up 20 percent, and for the first time we had a fully operating, responsive failure-reporting system in operation. 1973 saw the transfer of two top QC people into manufacturing management, and other talented people from lower QC ranks advanced. The test times on three different systems went below standards, and new goals were set for 1974.

---

result. In other words, what we must be able to say is what the person did that led to a result or to a set of results. To say that the person "showed initiative" is to say something useful but not specific. A more specific report would resemble the material in critical incidents; a detailed description of action ending in the result or even in the general actions roughly summarized in Cases 4–1 to 4–5 would be better than merely rating "initiative." To describe actions fully, you should develop more information about the environment in which the work was done. Only if you understand the ways in which other people and the impersonal environment supported or hindered the individual, can you make sense of the particular course the actions took. As you come to appreciate the reasons for actions taken, you will also begin to understand the ways in which the actions were superior or inferior.

Quantification of Action

If the foregoing analysis has shown that there is room for a person's actions to contribute to the results (which is to say that in

SOMETHING TO SHOW FOR THE YEAR'S EFFORTS

Our division was having problems getting our products produced and published when we needed them. I had been put in charge of this department as well as maintaining my job as product manager. A system was badly needed to help get our products when we needed them as well as to improve morale in the department.

I established a plan whereby each series had an editor in charge. Then all series had a staff that answered directly to the editor in charge. As the plan worked out, we were divided into six series, and each editor in charge reported directly to me. The art department was given a manager who also reported to me.

Since I had no technical knowledge of book production, I would not be of assistance on technical matters. That's what the art manager and series editors were for.

In summary, without increasing the size of the department, we published over 80 percent of our products on a predetermined schedule (compared with less than 30 percent in past years), and morale was much better because of the added responsibilities given to members of the department.

Table 4–2 Category 2, 3, 4, or 5 is satisfied), the next question is, "By what percentage did his or her actions produce those results?" This is not to suggest that a precise formula exists. Rather, it is to suggest the following principle: end results are determined by some combination of the person's action (P) and environmental factors (E). If the end result is "100 percent determined," then $P+E=100$. If you consider that the environment determines 30 percent of the results, the individual could at most determine 70 percent. This proportion would apply whether the results were good or bad. What is suggested here is not only that we must consider the role of the environment in all evaluation but that we should *not* quantify the quality of the actions. We should quantify only the *probability* with which the known actions led to the re-

THE IDEAL REPORT: RESULTS AND HOW WE GOT THEM

During January 1968 I was transferred to another branch. When I took over the store, sales were down, and the store was in the red. In reviewing the sales and profit structure with the DM, we found it almost impossible to return a profit with current sales where they were and the department sales breakdown where it was. The first thing I did was improve the service level at the front end during peak periods (happy customers). The next thing, after careful evaluation, was to change two section managers; I got both the replacements that I asked for. We then improved conditions in both sections. Within 3 months sales started to rise, offsetting the additional labor I had added, and the meat and dairy departments' percentage of store sales began to rise with the department manager changes and night pack-out in dairy. Sales have continued to rise to the present day, and when I left the store, it was number one in bottom-line profit percentage in the district and number two in the region.

---

sults. Probability numbers are merely certainty numbers. There are two ways to read this. One is that "100" means "I am 100 percent certain that what you did caused this result." It can also be read: "By 100, I mean that your actions determined the result *in toto*; you are solely accountable for them."

Qualitative Action

Thus we need not quantify actions such as initiative, persistence, and resourcefulness. Surely, however, action qualities are useful to know—at least we suggested so in earlier chapters. But they are not therefore ratable. The reason is that they are not what we pay people to do. We do not set up jobs for people to show initiative, persistence, or resourcefulness. We set up jobs for them to produce results or, more specifically, to produce actions which end in results. This is not to say that these action qualities are without merit; later in the chapter, we will show how they are to be used.

They are not to be quantified, however, and they should be deleted from forms. You may say, "But all I know is end results. I do not know what people are doing." If that is the case, you certainly cannot rate the qualities of their actions. It is difficult to know how you can rate the qualities of actions such as whether a person is delegating or motivating people if you have not observed actions that are classified in those ways. And if you have observed such actions, they are relevant only if they can be linked to results. Why rate initiative, for example, in a job for which it is a hazard to others? There are such jobs. In any case, you should rate, not whether the actions show adequate motivation of subordinates or delegation or initiative, but whether they produce the results for which the job exists. In summary, we rate performance in the following general way: performance equals the product of the value of results and the probability that the person's actions caused those results, or $R = V \times P$.

This formula enables us to see what is wrong with simply crediting a person with all the results in his or her operation. In Case 4–6 we see a good set of results but not many actions. This laundry list of objectives met or missed is not a good substitute for a narrative account such as Case 4–5.

THE POLITICS OF RATING

No one doubts that ratings are grossly influenced by favoritism and other kinds of unworthy politics. These sins are due not to lack of ethics or to bad feeling but rather to violation of a basic rule: people should be rated against only what they have been hired to do. It is obvious that we are describing a principle that will be difficult to follow. Inevitably, there will always be some residue of politics; our problem is not its elimination but its control.

Take a closer look as we describe how the game is played. There are easy indicators to show that the game *is* played. These vary from the pumping up of ratings at the favorable end so that year by year more employees get A ratings and fewer get D ratings—a

CASE
4–6

THE WEAKNESS OF MBO: RESULTS WITHOUT ACTION

The following are the objectives that I set in the areas of my responsibilities and the results for the year:

A. To reduce the waste in one type of department to 1 percent. It was reduced to 0.8 percent by the year date report.

B. To reduce the waste in another type of department to 3.5 percent. Figure obtained was 3.8 percent. Because of market conditions and boycotts, the availability of normal product flow had an influence on not obtaining goal.

C. To reduce a third department's waste to less than 3.5 percent. It was reduced below this figure.

D. To increase another department's sales from 11.5 to 15 percent. They were increased to 14 percent by greater merchandising and promotion to the special ethnic trade.

E. To institute receiving programs to ensure that correct merchandise was received. This was done, and the results were measured very favorably.

F. To evaluate department managers and review and evaluate performance. This was not done totally because of misscheduling of time on my part.

---

phenomenon that has been found not only in business but also in officers' fitness reports and in college grades. The game is played in the way that the personnel form itself is designed (usually for the convenience of the unmotivated raters). The most difficult and fine points of the game are shown by performers who defend themselves against unfavorable or unfair ratings by various maneuvers.

Let us consider Table 4–2 and the game that would be played if a boss and a subordinate did not like or trust one another. For any result or set of results, the boss's strategy would be to invoke Category P5 whenever the employee fails and Category P1 whenever the employee succeeds. By the same token, the boss would invoke the mirror image of these categories for his or her own role. The employee's defense is first to evade the evidence that there are in fact bad results while pointing to good ones. If there are inescapably bad results, the employee may argue the mirror image of the boss's position in terms of Table 4–2. That is, when successful, he or she adopts a Category P5 argument, and when unsuccessful a Category P1 argument. Depending on the sophistication of both parties, they may use in-between arguments. For example, the boss may attribute successes largely to business conditions (Category E2), while failures are ascribed to Categories E4 and E5. The defense by the subordinate is roughly the opposite within these middle categories, P2, P3, and P4.

Suppose corporate doctrine states, "Everyone is a member of a team." The boss may accept this proposition for successful results but may either deny the teamwork proposition for unsuccessful results or argue, "Results don't matter; it is only effort that counts." The general structure of these arguments, which we call "accountability games," is shown in Table 4–3.

Note that MBO (stating objectives in advance) alters the game of self-justification) but does not prevent it. MBO is really an argument about Category P3.

The Origin of Distal Qualities

In general, then, numbers are used in the political game in which each person wants to escape blame and receive credit. Depending on the relations among boss, subordinate, and organization, numbers are used in the following ways. The boss will attribute success to his or her own effective delegation (Area 2), choosing a person with the proper ability (Area 1), and motivating that person's effort (Area 3). Or the boss will attribute failure either to a person's lack of effort or ability, or both, since "of course" the task and the support structure (Area 2) were properly drawn up. The subordinate attributes success to his or her own actions in spite of environmental obstacles and, conversely, failure to those obstacles, which would have defeated anyone else's actions.

In attribution research, the performer is shown to describe and justify actions within a narrower time and space (environmental) frame than the observer does. The performer rates his or her actions on "proximate," or nearby, grounds, while observer goes further afield to explain what happened and evaluates action on "distal" grounds. The observer attributes traits such as initiative, intelligence, and persistence to the same actions about which the performer refuses to generalize.

Traits, which are the enduring characteristics of a person, are statements about Areas 1 and 3 of the micromap. Action, which is transient, is the content of Area 7. We believe only Areas 7 and 8 should be rated, and Area 7 rated against Area 8. An action's relevance is determined by Area 8.

According to this analysis, the rating form is designed from the standpoint of where the power lies: with the boss. We should find on the form various distal items to be rated which help prove the boss's case; this is the origin of traits such as effort and ability. The strategy of the subordinate, who is not in control of the items listed on the form, is to make all ratings more favorable or, if this fails, to ridicule the form itself. If this analysis is correct, the personnel rating form is designed to help the boss allocate blame and attribute traits, while the subordinate tries to escape blame and focus on immediate situations.

Statistical Solutions

Distal traits should not be quantified. If you have improperly quantified something, is it possible for statistical analysis to improve that use of numbers? We think not. However, there are statistical analyses which will reveal the extent to which you are in an impossible situation:

- *Halo or dunce-cap effect.* If you constantly attribute high or low ratings so that people tend to be rated generally high or low, you may be showing a halo or dunce-cap effect. This occurs if you use one rating as evidence for another rating, with

TABLE

4–3

ACCOUNTABILITY GAMES

What the boss can do if the subordinate seems successful

A. Lower the degree of subordinate accountability.

Effect: Increase degree to which results should be attributed to environment, including self.

B. Portray success as a team effort and raise the degree of accountability.

Effect: Praise one another's efforts, obscuring the possible role of environment.

C. Raise subordinate's degree on this particular success but decrease the number of other results called successful.

Effect: Can avoid further ability discussions until subordinate fails and then call for a review.

What the subordinate can do if he or she seems successful

A. Lower the degree of environmental accountability.

Effect: Call attention to own actions without appearing to do so.

B. Stress difficulty of environment, but then imply "I managed to overcome it."

Effect: Enhance one's own role.

C. Raise environmental accountability degree on other results but lower it on this particular one.

Effect: Focus evaluation on the subordinate's current strengths.

What the boss can do if the subordinate seems to fail

D. Share blame but lower accountability degree for both.

What the subordinate can do if he or she seems to fail

D. Call attention to difficulty of environment.

> *Effect:* Appear to give support while not giving up any points.

E. Act as if subordinate is not on the team.

> *Effect:* Avoid own blame and maximize accountability of subordinate.

General strategies for boss who does not yet know whether subordinate is succeeding or failing

F. Measure subordinate's performance on the basis of activity, good conduct, and costs.

> *Effect:* As these are not environmental criteria, the effect is to raise the accountability degree of the subordinate.

G. Create a climate of shared modesty as to results expected.

> *Effect:* Cautiously wait for environment to do something.

> *Effect:* Lower own accountability.

E. Detach self from organizational goals by denying the goals exist or undermine the boss.

> *Effect:* Lower accountability for failure.

General strategies for subordinate in a staff or other position the external results of which are not defined

F. Measure own performance on the basis of controllable factors such as own effort and costs.

> *Effect:* Increase one's ratings by appearing to work hard, stay within guidelines, supervise more people, and precisely control a larger budget. Ignore environment.

G. Lower own degree of accountability.

> *Effect:* Become more passive because accountability attributed to the environment is increased.

no observations to form the basis for a rating. In effect, you are talking to yourself.

- *Projection or mirror image.* If you rate a person high in initiative because you think him or her resourceful, what you are doing is merely expressing a theory. You are, as in the halo effect, using one of your opinions as the "evidence" for another opinion. Your theory has nothing to do with performance. Much research on trait ratings has shown that they represent such a use of the personnel rating form as a mirror image of the rater's theory.

The problem with the halo or dunce-cap effect and the projection of the rater's theory is serious because most of the ratings cannot be traced back to specific observations; there is no evidence for them. The rater observes one thing, say, a critical incident showing innovation, and from the justified rating of innovation makes the unjustified inferences of initiative, intelligence, and so on.

There are numerous other statistical problems with ratings, although some of them are not as serious as the above. If, for example, your ratings are unreliable, you may merely need more training in the categories rated. If you differ from other raters, you may be "anchoring" differently from them (starting your ratings from a different base line). These deficiencies can be remedied by more training and by discussion with other raters.

Statistical solutions cannot help if you are rating things that should not be rated at all.

THE MAGIC OF NUMBERS

Very large numbers of people believe that the stars affect us. They buy books which permit them to compute the consequences of birth dates. It is difficult for someone who does not believe in astrology to understand the origin of this belief. The history of magic is a long one which enables us to understand some of the obscure ways in which such strong beliefs arise. This history may help us see why businesses commonly allow themselves to be saddled with performance-rating systems as irrational as astrology.

The mere fact that you can compute consequences from your birth date following the instructions of a guidebook so impresses people that they do not care to question the origin of the guidebook. This is an old problem dating back at least a number of centuries. An ancient discipline called gematria contended that there was a computational relation between words and numbers. Each letter had a value. Using gematria, theologians "proved" that the beast of the Book of Revelation had a number: it turned out to be 666. Then a Catholic writer named Bungus succeeded in showing that this also was the number of Martin Luther's name. Luther's defense was to "prove" that 666 was the proper forecast of the duration of the papacy, whose end was therefore at hand, and thus he "got the number" of the Roman Catholic Church.

The history of numbers in industrial psychology is a long one, if not dating quite as far back as gematria. The decisive theory causing much of the mischief was perhaps Edward Lee Thorndike's argument that everything existing must exist in some amount and therefore can be measured. If a person has enough of a trait to say that he or she has *some,* then we can ask "How much?" Thus an introverted person must have a certain "amount" of introversion. In this way, by a more sophisticated version of gematria, people's traits were expressed in numbers. It was then a small step to putting trait scores in personnel files.

And there they sit today: legal time bombs in equal-opportunity cases if you base decisions on these scores unless you can cross-examine their meaning as numbers, showing that they refer not to the theories of your raters but to critical incidents and other documented performance.

It is true that there are legitimate mysteries in mathematics and great power in using numbers in science, but there are enough mysteries and paradoxes in numbers without inventing additional ones by numbering people and their traits, at least for performance analysis.

WHAT TO DO WITH TRAITS

Nevertheless, people show enduring characteristics, and some of these are relevant to work. Who can doubt that persistence, initiative, and decisiveness, all characteristics on our much-abused federal form, are important? We have argued that you should not quantify traits unless, in rare instances, you are paying persons to show their traits. It is difficult (though possible) to imagine a job in which a personality trait is the end product or output. For the overwhelming majority of jobs, we need to use another way of representing traits. There is a simple answer: represent traits by using plain language.

The recommendation is to use language in its traditional, natural, and very powerful way. In characterizing a person, language describes traits in a dichotomous fashion: a person shows "initiative" or does not. If this is not sufficient, use qualifying adjectives. Traits, however, do not belong on performance-rating forms. Instead, we shall outline briefly the natural way to use traits in ordinary language.

What numbers do best is to quantify tangible values and probabilities. What numbers do worst is to quantify the subtlety of human behavior. What language does worst is to sum up the essentials of complex technology. What language does best is to characterize behavior, feelings, the context of action, its history, and its consequences. What we should do, therefore, is not only to *quantify* output and its causes but also to *describe* action, the conditions under which it occurs, and other such factors which make up what was earlier defined as a critical incident or a longer performance account. On the micromap, language is used to characterize all areas, while numbers are useful only in the central ones, Areas 7 and 8. For example, Area 1 refers to enduring personal qualities concerned with ability: we should describe ability in plain language; we should not quantify it. In other words, after an episode of performance has been written in plain narrative language, we describe only the abilities, effort, relations to the environment, and the like shown in that incident. However, these make more

TOWARD THE PROPER COORDINATION OF WORDS AND NUMBERS

Here are some suggested dos and don'ts:

Do	Don't
1. Rate what you hire a person to do: outputs.	1. Do not use traditional personnel forms. The only response to these forms which makes sense usually is evasion.
2. Consider the strength of external causes affecting results.	2. Do not play the charade of rating or valuing things which have not been observed.
3. Quantify the influence of the person's actions on those results.	3. Do not employ number magic.
4. Use words to produce the original working account and reason about its meaning.	4. Do not grade good conduct or other traits.
5. If you are poor in using language, learn how to use it better.	5. Do not overestimate the output measures. They will not speak for themselves; that is, they require an organic inquiry to elucidate their meaning.

sense when described *organically* in relation to one another than when split into traits.

What use is made of trait lists such as that in the sample federal form? Is this list not useful to define qualities such as resourcefulness, decisiveness, and delegation? Traits are preformed thoughts about a person. When used as substitutes for observation and narrative accounts, they are secondhand. They are cheap substitutes. Their popularity perhaps is due to American resistance to using written language (it is hard work to look for the causes of action) and to the hurried character of a modern supervisor's work. The technical manager may be limited in vocabulary and seek convenient preformed thoughts, preferring to rate people rather than describe what he or she sees and thinks. In this chapter we have tried to show that such shortcuts are illegitimate.

Obviously, it is strongly recommended that you redesign your performance-rating procedures around organic reasoning. No number can create new knowledge. The power of a number lies in its assistance to reason, not in its substitute for information. Only a knowledgeable person can quantify. Politics in performance rating is inevitable but controllable. A search for control will not be easy, but you can begin by discovering ways in which your present procedures lead the boss to fake it and the subordinate to lie.

5

TALKING YOURSELF
INTO GOOD JUDGMENT

You've heard the saying "No one ever listened himself into trouble, but people often talk themselves into it." It is also true that people talk themselves into bad judgment about others. In this chapter we're concerned with how to use words in judging performance. The essence of the problem is that we use the same words to describe what we see that we do to project what we feel, and this mixing of facts and values greatly complicates making sense about people. It would be easy enough to say, "Stop using value-loaded words." Pure behaviorists seem to recommend this. We think their recommendation goes too far, but there is merit in the idea that language must start with what can be seen and proved about other people.

We must learn to be suspicious of words. Using words to describe people often resembles looking out at the world through a dirty window. Words have limitations in carrying meaning. There are particular words which are notoriously difficult—words which carry bias. Other words, while not so obviously biased, conceal reality behind symbols which we take for granted but which cannot stand the test of fact. Still other language is troublesome because we mix statements about a person's attitudes with statements about his or her performance.

Words Easy to Criticize

These words we shall call "cheaptalk," because they come to mind all too easily out of our prejudices. Instead of saying that a person is not promotable because he or she is a poor performer (legitimate), cheaptalk says that person is not promotable because he or she is black (illegal). Only a fool makes such statements these days about blacks, women, and other members of protected classes. Bias has moved underground in language, so these obviously legally liable statements do not require our attention here. Anyone who does not know from lawyers what his or her legal liability is by now is not going to learn it from this book.

A less obvious version of cheaptalk falls under the heading of using symbols instead of reality. For example, in advertising the man of distinction drinks our whiskey, drives a fancy car, is dressed to perfection, and otherwise looks good. These are symbols. We all know that such a man may or may not be a top performer. But he looks to some people as if he *would* be. There are businesses that hire such symbols or figureheads. There's nothing wrong with looking well, dressing well, or driving a Mercedes-Benz. One can as easily be a top performer who looks or dresses well or drives an expensive car as a person who does not, but in very few jobs would these things have anything whatsoever to do with performance. Table 5–1 lists a number of symbols commonly used as a substitute for observation and relevant facts. That table, however, has two columns. Notice the merits on the left, which include commonly accepted symbols such as we have mentioned. On the right are demerits which the reader may find difficult to consider as such. These are general signs of social disfavor. They may have nothing to do with performance on the job, but it is difficult to learn to use language without such demerits.

THE PROBLEM WITH CHEAPTALK

Cheaptalk (using general merit or demerit to describe a person) substitutes symbol for fact. In its extreme form, this substitution is

TABLE

5-1

THE SOCIAL MERIT AND DEMERIT SYSTEM

Consider a person better qualified for a good job if he or she meets the following criteria	*Consider a person not qualified for a good job if the following are true*
Anglo dialect	Complexion that looks "different"
Athletic appearance (if male)	Poor credit rating
Attendance at "best" schools (mine)	Ethnic dialect
Demographic criteria: age, gender, race, and so on	Youth in a red-lined or high-crime area
High earnings	Low grades
Education	Low test scores
Father in status occupation	Need for a job
Children (if male)	Physical handicap
Stable job history	Heavy build
Married status (if male)	Too much seniority
Seniority up to a point	Too short stature (if male)
Well-dressed appearance	Too tall stature (if female)

a form of madness. In business, it is a cause of inexact or irrelevant judgment of people. Let us illustrate.

You are a scout for a professional football team. You have watched Jones and Smith, two candidates for tackle. You have seen them play, block, tackle, and endure injury, and you have a pocket full of statistics on how well they have performed. When you give your recommendation on which tackle to draft, will you draw from the foregoing, or will you say things like the following?

- Jones has his master's degree; Smith doesn't.

- Jones has an A average, while Smith has only a C average.

- Jones is extremely well dressed and has a military bearing; Smith isn't and doesn't.

- Smith got twenty-five traffic tickets last year.

- Smith is a poor credit risk.

- Smith went to the wrong college. Most of the people on our team went to Northwestern, whereas Smith went to a college we never heard of.

- Jones belongs to the right political party.

- Smith is ugly.

- Smith stutters.

- Jones gives you a handshake which is firm and dry and looks you in the eye.

These statements are a caricature of cheaptalk. You may think them a joke, but there are a number of business firms that hire or promote people by using such criteria to distinguish Jones from Smith rather than by using realistic ones like those first listed (blocking, tackling, enduring injury).

On one occasion, we attempted to use trait lists (including such words as *cooperative, tactful,* and *aggressive*) to show managers how to measure their insights into others. The experiment produced peculiar results. Each manager described a close friend from the group and also someone he did not know well, if at all. Each description was compared with what the person described said about himself; the similarity was expected to show greater insight into the friend's character. Actually, there was no difference. The manager's insight was as great into the "stranger" whom he had scarcely observed as into the friend he thought he knew. One inference is that such trait descriptions convey very little information about a person. The managers perhaps knew their friends well, but trait ratings are too superficial to demonstrate their knowledge.

To remove such words from our language would be almost to speak without nouns in judging persons. This seems to be the recommendation of Mischel (1968). Instead of saying what a person *is* or what characteristics the person *has*, we should simply describe what that person *does*. Would this not keep us closer to reality, since in any case what we observe is what people do? While we do not think traits can so easily be censored, the proposal does focus our attention upon ways to make language more realistic.

THE LADDER OF ABSTRACTION

If we describe only behavior, won't we get down to earth and limit what we say to what we observe? While behavioral analysis is not enough, this down-to-earth suggestion offers us a clue for doing as the general semanticist Alfred Korzybski long ago urged: get low on the ladder of abstraction when there is confusion in the use of symbols. Since the publication of Korzybski's book *Science and Sanity* (1933), others have eloquently called for clearing up the confusions of words and using certain devices for teaching and communicating. These devices have been elaborated and advocated by Wendell Johnson, S. I. Hayakawa, Irving Lee, and others, writing over the last quarter century. One such fundamental idea is not to lose the tie between the symbol and the events it represents. For example, if you talk about an employee who is "untrustworthy" but cannot give any examples or evidence for the characterization, you have lost touch with reality.

You should test your abstractions about another person against facts and learn to describe in a way that can be so tested. This means using the abstraction ladder properly. The ladder rests on the ground (the original reality you observed) and has these rungs:

Zero level: Ground of original fact

Rung 1: The observations you choose to note and remember

Rung 2: What you choose to say in describing these observations

Rung 3: Generalizations you make, such as saying that what you have seen is "always the case" or "usually the case" with this person

Rung 4
and higher: Still more sweeping conclusions that these generalizations lead you to make

The higher rungs are farther from the ground of reality. They are also riskier in the sense of losing touch with reality. And, the more rungs you are up, the more trouble it is to move down the ladder and touch earth, where your strength is according to ancient myth. The following rules or devices prevent loss of touch with reality and encourage consciousness of the ladder of abstraction (Figure 5-1). These devices are fundamental to this book; you first encountered them explicitly in Chapter 2, but they appear frequently throughout.

Dating and Indexing

What is real about a person always is what occurred at a particular time and place or consists of many such instances. Learning to give examples in terms of specific incidents is a discipline which fosters dating and indexing. The question resembles the courtroom question "Where were you on the night of January 16?" Between Rungs 2 and 3 you lose place and time. That is a big loss, and you should learn to recognize it when it happens.

"Is Not"

Korzybski traced much semantic madness to the use of word forms such as *is* for "identity." These word forms lead us to classify a person as "a woman," "an engineer," or "a carpenter." Such a classification is so factual that it seemingly poses no problem of verification. But the problem is not the fact but the fact's implications: they represent a leap to Rung 3 or Rung 4 (generali-

Figure
5-1

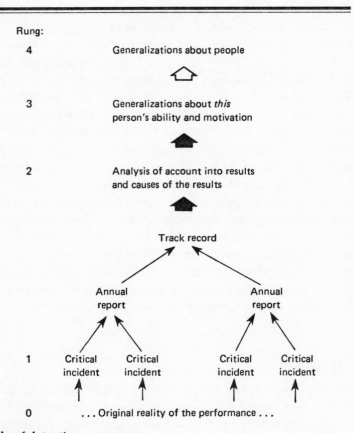

Rung:

4   Generalizations about people

3   Generalizations about *this* person's ability and motivation

2   Analysis of account into results and causes of the results

Track record

Annual report   Annual report

1   Critical incident   Critical incident   Critical incident   Critical incident

0   . . . Original reality of the performance . . .

Ladder of abstraction.

zations) from the original reality with no reasoning in between. This is a woman (observed fact), but we don't have to observe any of her behavior (Rung 1), or discuss it (Rung 2), or think about it (Rung 3). We just go directly from the fact of sex to some sweeping conclusion (Rung 4 or higher). We therefore draw conclusions which have nothing whatsoever to do with the individual *behavior* of the person. Conclusions are drawn about one person merely by classifying that person in a larger category.

The semantically protective device is to learn to use the word form *is not* to show that no one category can ever say all there is to say about anyone. Try the following. Take Leroy Jones and, in the face of his blackness, say, "Leroy Jones is not black." Take Jane Fonda and say, "Jane Fonda is not a woman." Take your child and say, "Jack is not my son." The point is that more can always be said about Leroy Jones than that he "is" black. Jane Fonda "is" more than a woman. Jack "is" more than a son. You already know all that. But Korzybski had no quarrel with what you consciously know. It was *assumptions* that general semantics considered the source of our common madness. If you observe, describe, and decide about Leroy Jones as if being black is all there is to say, as if Jane Fonda is merely woman, and as if Jack is nothing but your son, you are out of touch. You will reify your categories. You will stop thinking behavior and stop seeing what is dynamically there: the changing process that a person is will pass you by because you have locked up your thoughts in a static set of conclusions.

"Is Not All"

Closely related to the "is" of identity is the "not all" protective device. The journal *ETC.* was named for this device. The drill to escape abstractions and categories is to add the term "et cetera" at the end of sentences. It is hoped that this encourages you to:

- Accept that the person is changing. Your description cannot be all there is and must be updated in the future.

- Accept the fallibility of your conclusions.

- Develop the healthy interest of wanting to observe more than you have observed in the past.

GOING UP AND DOWN THE LADDER

So far the recommendations have seemed to say: "Get more conservative, behavioristic, and tough-minded in the words you lay on people." That's right, but it's not enough if you must make long-range decisions based on identifying persisting characteristics. Someone in our society must deal more effectively with the following questions:

- Will this scientist, if given special research funds, produce major research discoveries?

- Will this candidate, if elected, serve the public well?

- Will this chief executive put our company in the black?

In answering these questions, you must be able to move up the abstraction ladder. The solution, then, is to be able to move *up* and *down* the ladder, not just to seek objectivity by making no generalizations at all. Going down, you become more behavioristic. The parole board that turns down the applicant must be able to say why. The "why" must consist of more than a "gut feeling" for the case; it must cite behavioral observations as the basis or evidence for its unfavorable forecast. The parole board that lets a known killer out must be able to defend its conclusions. The defense of a decision, then, always involves behavioral observation. But you must be more than an observer to be a decision maker.

There is a further sense in which strict tough-mindedness must be rejected. According to the premises of this book, a responsible judge must be empathic, detecting the feelings expressed in behavior and not only the behavior. Empathy is a necessary part of the general attempt to make sense of significant behavior. Can we really make sense if we cannot estimate how the performer defined his or her situation?

CONVERTING CHEAPTALK TO HUMAN ACCOUNTS

We have diagnosed the problem and found that the solution is being able to go up and down the abstraction ladder. Cheaptalk quickly jumps up the ladder and uses symbolic abstractions without criticism or foundation. Simply learning to use carefully defined traits is no remedy for cheaptalk. The remedy must include:

- Ways to use behavioral evidence to reach conclusions or to explain where they come from

- Ways to use empathy as well as behavior so that we get the person's help in making sense of what we observe

The personnel report, medical history, superficial novel, and offensive newspaper story all need to delete cheaptalk and become more humanistic. Following the remedy outlined above, writing and talking would show the characteristics of humanistic behaviorism. This is one of the main reasons for learning how to use working accounts rather than simple business reports (Case 5-1).

THE PROBLEM OF ATTITUDE

Many seek to hire people with the "proper attitude." The language of this phrase poses particular problems. First, attitudes are difficult to judge, although as we shall find, there are some ways to do so. Even so, you should not judge attitudes except as part of your effort to make sense of and improve performance. Attitudes fail the test question, "Do we have this job for people to display their attitudes?" It is difficult to think of displaying an attitude as the purpose of a job. The purpose of a job is to produce some kind of business result. An attitude may be necessary for producing a business result, but it is not in itself one of the results for which a business or a job within a business exists. Nervertheless, we must cope with rather than complain about attitudes (Case 5-2).

A HUMANISTIC ACCOUNT BY A TOP OBSERVER

HOTS MICHAELS: "Do you have a favorite tune? Here's an oldie." He plays "As Time Goes By." The piano bar is fairly crowded. The drinking is casual. It is early evening at the downtown hotel. Once it was a favorite gathering place for the city's sporting crowd, politicians, and strangers looking for action. It will be razed this year to make way for a modern high rise.

He started here in 1952. He refers to a mutual friend, who has since died. "Chet and I began the whole thing. The first piano bar was in this hotel. Now every tavern and saloon has one." There is a jukebox in the room. Its loudness envelops all during the piano breaks.

He works five nights a week, from five-thirty to "around midnight. If there's a crowd, I keep going. I might play many hours in a row. I take a break when it's empty." There are frequent phone calls for him, interrupting the conversation.

"Piano playing is incidental to this place. It's kind of background music for talking. Businessmen talking deals. Out-of-town visitors. Occasionally you get some people interested in hearing a certain type of song, and you entertain them. I never took any lessons. I play strictly by ear. I'm lucky I can read titles. (Laughs.)

"Over the years I get to know people. They'll hit the piano bar and we'll talk back and forth. A second group will move in, strangers. They might be from small towns and they want to know what's happening. You have close contact with people. This petrifies some piano players, so they play with bands. I never played with a band because I wasn't qualified.

"Late business is a thing of the past. People don't stay down as late as they used to after work. The local people will have their drinks and go home. At one time they stayed down five, six hours. And they don't come down like they used to. They have places out in the suburbs. . . ."

From Studs Terkel, *Working: People Talk about What They Do All Day and How They Feel about What They Do.* New York: © Pantheon Books, a Division of Random House, Inc., 1977, 250.

COPING WITH A COLLEAGUE'S ATTITUDE

In 1968 or 1969 I supervised the electronics development for a computer-controlled audio recorder. It was a large program involving many people, both employees and contract personnel. One day, after a highly respected contract engineer had repeatedly been late and shown a lackadaisical attitude, I found it necessary to complain to the department manager. When the engineer found out about it, he came to me in the middle of a large, busy lab and became extremely angry, shouting loudly that that hadn't been necessary and calling me names such as "crybaby." With some difficulty I retained my outward composure and suggested that he get back to work. Several witnesses among the rather large crowd later said they were even more surprised than I that I had held my temper. This experience provided the incentive to become better at self-control.

Types of Attitudes

For reasons of research (of Edward E. Lawler, Victor Vroom, and others) we are concerned primarily with three attitudes. Performance requires such assumptions by the person as the following:

- "If I try, I am likely to succeed"—confident expectation.
- "If I succeed, I will be rewarded"—trust in the organization.
- "If I do this work, I will enjoy it"—the work appears worth doing.

If a person is saying things or implying an attitude like any of these three, the basis exists for good performance. But suppose the person is not.

- On the micromap, confidence results from past experience of ability in similar tasks and a feeling of good support from the boss. These are the two roots of confidence. The micromap suggests that a problem of competence has several potential solutions:

1. Find areas of past experience which justify greater confidence on the part of the person (this is more the task of the counselor than of the boss).

2. Reduce the difficulty of the task until it is at the individual's competence level.

3. Give more solid assurance of support in the task.

- On the micromap, the expectation that success will bring long-term benefits implies a good fit between the job setting and a person's needs. This analysis suggests that if this attitudinal problem exists the following things can be done:

1. Probe further into the individual's needs to find those that would be satisfied by this job. (Again, this may be a task for a job counselor rather than for the boss.)

2. Renegotiate the person's long-range expectations so that either they can be met more realistically or the company gives firmer assurances that they will be met.

3. Give more immediate rewards whenever the individual is successful. The rewards, of course, are for needs that the individual actually has rather than needs that someone else attributes to him or her.

- If the third attitudinal problem, that the individual does not enjoy the work, exists, there are several options:

1. The job itself can be enriched so that it meets more needs.

2. It is common to change external conditions by providing better working surroundings, coffee breaks, and more frequent contact with the boss (or less frequent supervision). Whether such changes will be worthwhile depends on the needs.

3. The individual can be transferred to another job. While no one will enjoy every job, we believe every job has some takers. Few of us can endure even the thought of construction labor eighty stories high, but one Indian tribe is thought to value this work as a challenge to manhood.

PRODUCTIVITY VERSUS ATTITUDE

In 1973 I was called into the boss's office, where he, the night superintendent, and my boss's boss were present. I was (and still am) foreman for two secondary machine departments consisting of 145 people in a three-shift operation. One of my men, Zeke, had been active in the last union organizing campaign. Zeke works the second shift.

Zeke is a hard worker, with the highest productivity of my two departments, excellent attendance, and higher-than-average incidence of rework for his group, and he has a strong sense of what is fair and honest. On this last point, if Zeke comes to me with something that is not right, I know he has done his homework and is right, that it is of a serious nature, and that he has dealt unsuccessfully with the chain of command between us.

In the meeting with my superiors I was told another union drive was in progress and I would earn my first big star the day I fired Zeke. I was to watch him very closely for any infractions. I told the men of my understanding of Zeke's record, which they could not deny, and stated there was no cause for termination at this time. I have been pointedly reminded of my "duty" by my superiors on two occasions since.

The next night after the meeting when I was making my rounds, Zeke remarked that he didn't want to go into detail but thanked me very much and offered that any time I needed any of the more disliked jobs done just to let him know. I told no one of the meeting except my father, so Zeke's knowledge of what transpired at the meeting baffles me.

The meeting itself greatly depressed me because quite a bit of pressure was put on me to do something I thought to be dishonest. Also, the bosses were very aggressive in trying to get me to commit myself to disliking Zeke and trying to "get him." I wouldn't do it. Zeke will be treated like everyone else.

Many of us believe "dirty" jobs are hard to fill. But it is good to remember that some people like to do autopsies.

Research on such expectations has been reported only in recent years. It is too early to draw general conclusions except to suggest that the first attitude, expecting to succeed, has more predictable effects than the other two. Expecting to succeed plus one of the other two attitudes appears to be a must for generating action, but it is not at all clear that expecting to benefit and expecting to enjoy are always compatible. For example, one research study showed that a person in volunteer work, in which no tangible benefits are paid for success, may receive a high degree of intrinsic satisfaction in the work. If you suddenly start paying that individual for the same work, thus conferring a tangible benefit, interest in payment suddenly becomes very important, and intrinsic satisfaction drops. This is a curious psychological finding which we neither understand nor can be certain is generally true. Nevertheless, it illustrates the point that there are mysteries about job attitudes and that you should not be glib.

WHAT TO DO ABOUT ATTITUDES

We have already said what *not* to do about attitudes: don't rate them. People should not be hired, promoted, rewarded, fired, or otherwise judged for attitudes (Case 5-3). What we should do is to attempt to influence those attitudes, to *build* them. How can we do this? The following procedure has been found by many managers to give them valuable insight into the kinds of attitudes that exist in their organizations and to indicate areas in which negotiation with employees will change attitudes favorably.

Table 5-2 is a sample form on role conflict. The aim of this procedure is to determine where boss and subordinate differ in their perception of the subordinate's job. The steps in this procedure are:

1. Define six to eight duties making up the subordinate's job. These should include all significant duties as well as duties for which it is possible to establish criteria for evaluation.

2. Write these duties on the form.

TABLE
5-2

SAMPLE OF ROLE CONFLICT

Husband and wife independently ranked the following role statements, 1 being highest.

Wife's role	Importance		Difficulty		Liking	
	Wife	Husband	Wife	Husband	Wife	Husband
A. Keeping household accounts	7	8	5	1	7	7
B. Planning menus	4	4	7	6	6	6
C. Shopping for the household	5	5	6	5	5	3
D. Sexual relations*	6	2	3	8	4	1
E. Long-range financial planning	8	6	1	3	8	8
F. Working in own career*	1	7	2	4	1	5
G. Talking with husband	2	1	4	7	2	2
H. Cooking	3.	3	8	2	3	4

NOTES:

1. Areas in which clarification would be advised are marked*.

2. Role statements pertain to wife, as seen by either wife or husband. (A similar approach would be used to describe husband's role but is not shown here.)

3. Conflict would be more accurately estimated by squaring the differences. Thus the conflict over the importance of Item F is 6 points, or 2 points more than over sex. Squared, F shows 36 points, many times larger than any other conflict in importance.

3. Make a copy; have boss and subordinate *independently* rank the duties for each of the following three characteristics:

   a. Rank the duties for difficulty: 1 is given to the duty on which the subordinate is most likely to succeed, 2 to the next duty, and so on, down to 8, the most difficult for that particular subordinate.

   b. Then rank the same duties according to whether success will have a payoff. Assign 1 to the duty for which boss or subordinate is willing to say "If you succeed in this task, the company will know it and most strongly reward you," and so on, down to 8, the duty for which there is least expectation of tangible benefit.

   c. Rank the duties from 1 to 8 according to whether the subordinate likes to perform the particular duty (1 is the task or duty most liked, and 8 the one most rejected).

4. Compare rankings between boss and subordinate on each of the scales *a, b,* and *c.* A difference of 3 or more indicates a significant role-conflict area. A total difference of 24 points means a significant across-the-board role conflict.

5. Renegotiate the job. This means concentrating on areas with significant discrepancies or on the job as a whole if the sum of discrepancies is 16 or more.

What does it mean to negotiate a job? In the old days a supervisor assigned work. It would seem that since the supervisor has authority to do this, *negotiate* is the wrong word. The problem is that research has repeatedly shown that discrepancies in perception of work are so great that the traditional forms of delegation are obviously inadequate. Furthermore, the differences between subordinate and boss, in authority or salary or education, are now sometimes so slight that the two feel equal. Finally, what is known as participative management calls for communication between equals insofar as possible. Even if the authority differences are tolerable, it is rare that a person in authority can demand or direct another person's attitude to change. Hence we use the word *negotiation.*

Negotiation here means a number of things. First, it means to

NEGOTIATION CAN BACKFIRE

Two years ago I was given an assignment to analyze the wholesaling activities of one of my dealers. I had stayed up until after midnight drawing charts, putting figures together, etc. I made the preliminary presentation to the parts manager only, since the dealer was not in. On my follow-up call I presented my analysis to the dealer, pointing out certain areas of weakness. As a result, the parts manager thought I was after his job and became irrational to the point of threatening to throw me out physically. We both confronted the dealer and reviewed the situation. The end result was that the parts manager quit.

PEOPLE WANT FEEDBACK FROM YOU

My lack of outward emotion has many times been misinterpreted as a lack of caring. One incident that comes to mind was in 1969. As a department manager, I had just been told by my district manager that my department's gross profit had come back terrible. I acknowledged the fact and was thinking of any possible way it could be a mistake when he screamed, "Look at you! You don't even care!" I'll never forget the words. I realized then that people, both bosses and subordinates, look for reaction but still find it difficult to get overemotional.

clarify why the difference in perception exists. This alone may be sufficient to change a point of view, but sometimes it is not, as in Case 5-4. Usually the discussion of discrepancies will then proceed in a natural way, and it need not be outlined here. Topics often brought up include the following: "If we differ as to the difficulty of tasks, what have we done to make the hardest parts easier, for example, through greater support from above?" "If we differ as to promotion chances, what can a subordinate hear which will provide greater assurance?" "If we differ as to what is interesting about this job, what can we do about the nature of the job to give it greater appeal?" Sometimes the answer to the last question is greater freedom to determine working conditions or hours, and sometimes it is greater freedom to do the work as the subordinate thinks it should be done.

Second, negotiation is not just an exchange of information; it is an exchange of *energy*. Labor relations people know what that means. An illustration is in Case 5-5. This exchange clarifies priorities through the district manager's emotion, while the department manager's nonemotional manner misleads the district manager about the performer's true practices.

Do	Don't
1. Use low-level-of-abstraction terms, down-to-earth words describing performance.	1. Use demographic categories (older, female, black, etc.) as a substitute for describing performance.
2. Describe what people are doing rather than your feelings about them.	2. Use résumés instead of track records of performance.
3. Use plain language, not "psychobabble."	3. Substitute status symbols for substance.
4. Concern yourself with building attitudes.	4. Use terms like "qualified" or "unqualified" which cannot be traced back to actual performance.
5. Detect and correct the problems in the job contract (the role).	5. Rate attitudes.

6

WHY NOT PROMOTE THE PERFORMER?

If you apply what has been covered in previous chapters, you should now know something more about who is performing well and why. You should be able to identify talent; why not promote it? Why not reverse the trend that the Peter principle claims is true of big organizations—that they promote people until it is obvious those people cannot go further, if indeed they have not already exceeded their limits?

Not everyone agrees it is obvious that one should promote top performers. There are some powerful arguments against this promotion. Chief among these is that jobs differ. The top sales representative will not necessarily make a top sales manager. The argument goes that the sales manager needs skills that cannot be judged at the level of a sales representative. We shall consider the merits of this argument, although they are not enough to justify the extreme of ignoring performance altogether. A more serious argument against our proposal is that few bosses know who is performing well or that, if they do know, few know why. This argument becomes more impressive in large corporations or in cases in which boss and subordinates are separated geographically. Performance review, according to earlier chapters, produces so little real information that track record promotions are impossible. When the track record is not well known, promotions are based on other factors. What are they? They include options such as the "old boy" network, bureaucratic ratings, and psychological systems of varying degrees of sophistication. To them all we prefer the track record. Admittedly it requires modifications to overcome the limitations already noted.

What is the track record? It is the manager's life of accomplishments and defeats, including well-founded explanations. These explanations should show the person's resources as a manager and his or her limitations and values. A company can make a defensible promotion only if it has full knowledge of this track record. It is obvious that this knowledge is in the company's interest. What is not so obvious is that few companies possess it. To put companies in a position of having full knowledge of the track records of all serious candidates is a difficult task even though we regard it as ethically imperative. While the task is difficult, however, it has favorable side effects on other aspects of company operations. Chief among these is the boost to the morale of high performers; even if the high performers are disliked, the side effects from rewarding productivity should be obvious.

TRACK RECORD PROMOTION

Most managers can recite a series of accomplishments of which they feel proud and with which they can justify their take-home pay. These results may be sales, the resolution of problems in labor relations, the maintenance of good customer relations, the weathering of financial crises, the introduction of new products, or a fight for personnel policies. A manager with such results feels that he or she has made a real contribution. Nevertheless, such a list of accomplishments, however factual, is not enough.

It is the explanation of these results which is missing. Other managers may dispute that the particular manager caused the results, which might have occurred without his or her contribution, or the manager may have obstructed an event and been overridden by another, who should instead be credited with the good results.

REVIEWING HIS TRACK RECORD TAUGHT HIM SOMETHING

The first 6 months of 1972 I spent in the management training program. This was followed by a major task in the Union City store. That store had the highest waste in the company, $127,000 per quarter. My job was to do whatever was necessary to cut the shrinkage (food loss) to less than $50,000. I was able to do this. The biggest problem was that I showed little concern for people and forced them to do things my way. I did not take the time to develop them. I was concerned only with meeting the challenge in the shortest possible time. People in this store either loved me or hated me.

We therefore must find ways to interrogate the track record to obtain the context within which to understand the results.

Every track record is earned against a given set of costs. "Costs" refer not only to resources consumed but to other results forgone for the sake of the ones listed. Moreover (and this point will confuse many), the track record should include gains achieved through defeats. There is such a thing as a strategic loss—a result which, while technically a cost in a given year, can be expected to have a longer-term payoff. Included in this category are defeats which teach a manager or even an organization a needed lesson (Case 6–1). Thus what begins as a simple personal balance sheet of accomplishments and defeats turns out to be far more complicated and interesting. At an intellectual level, the interest resembles the fascination of a detective story or even of a historical reconstruction. At a social level, the interest lies in negotiating the meaning of an account with another person. There is a political level of interest: persuading an organization to forgo some of its traditions which support the "buddy system" of ratings and to substitute a more adult system such as track records. The political challenge is so great as to constitute perhaps the supreme challenge confronting a new corporate president. The specific steps required to move an organization from its former system of promotion to a track record system would include the following:

1. Inform the organization that promotions will be based on track records.

2. Train everyone in reconstructing and analyzing track records.

3. When positions become open, encourage candidates to present their track records.

4. Verify these records in their most critical, factual aspects.

5. Appoint a panel (trained as recommended above) to appraise these verified track records against the requirements of the positions to be filled.

This bland summary of the steps to be taken conceals the internal forces present in any large social system which, unless understood, will make a mockery of an organization's program.

A LOOK AT THE OPTIONS

We should first understand the strong appeal of competing options. While the track record system may sound like common sense, there are a number of alternative systems. There must be some reason for their existence. In general, many organizations believe that they have a track record system when they do not. For example, performance ratings cannot measure operating results; rather they measure the conclusions of someone who may or may not have made a detailed interrogation about the causes of the results. For another example, financial results are sometimes mistaken for track records. It is true that financial results are among the most important results included in a track record, but without careful examination they may be attributed to the wrong manager.

The options are to continue prevailing systems of promotion, to substitute for them the track record system, or gradually to make a transition to the track record system. Alternative systems include:

Political system. Promote those who are well regarded and acceptable at the top or in the organization generally.

Bureaucratic system. Promote those who have been accredited through a standardized procedure widely understood in the organization.

Use of personal qualities. Promote those who look like, sound like, and manage like the persons you want in the job.

Use of good conduct. Promote those whose behavior adheres to agreed-on standards.

These four systems or combinations of them are widespread. They have important organizational advantages, suggested by the way they've been defined. What, therefore, is wrong with them, and how do they defeat the track record system, in which talent would rise to the top of the pyramid?

Here we pause to make a note to our readers. Most readers have moved up in the pyramid and may resent Lawrence J. Peter's suggestion that the cream has not risen to the top of the bottle. The only way we can salvage your egos is to suggest that you may possess promotable qualities in the sense of having good track records and yet move up the pyramid for the wrong reasons. There is nothing incompatible with having a good track record and being politically adept, between having a good track record and having good bureaucratic relations, and so forth.

POLITICS

The corporation is a place of power in both the good and the bad sense. People must influence policies, not merely decide them. The injection of the term "influence" immediately brings in politics, which can be for good or for evil. With the increase in the number of staff specialties, the importance of influence has changed rather than diminished. For example, the autocratic line manager influenced perhaps in a simple way. Now, with so many staff specialties, we have many different kinds of influence. The game of poli-

POLITICS MADE PHIL A SCAPEGOAT

Phil Roth was a top engineer who made the transition to management, but he never lost sight of technical innovation as the lifeblood of the company, as he saw it. He stuck his neck out on some questionable investments in research: the KV-4 engine eventually was the result. A cool billion in sales was the payoff by the time the dust settled on that one innovation. Phil was also known as a firm manager who got things done. Thus the home office tapped Phil to take over the Midwestern division, which had been steadily losing money for 6 years under three general managers. They gave Phil 6 months to turn this major operation around. His methods were a bit rough, and he had never been known as a diplomat. The division *was* turned around in 6 months, but the research engineering department quit en masse. Phil was in Siberia. He finally left, for a better job paying double what he was getting as general manager. A consultant investigated this case and wrote the company: "Phil's methods worked, and the engineers quit because his 6-month deadline forced tactics on him he would not otherwise have used. It was the home office's deadline which caused the problem. You should try to keep Phil."

tics has merely changed. It has not departed. Since influence is necessary in the modern corporation, we can make a good case for using political arithmetic in adding up the points for promotion candidates. Why not promote a manager who has a reputation for using influence to get results? The following flaws appear to be inherent in any political system:

- Political systems do not take the time to decide whether a manager actually caused the results attributed to him or her. Rather, the person who possesses prestige is *assumed* to have caused all favorable results in his or her department and succeeds in disowning bad results by attributing them to subordinates. To say the least, this situation is destructive (Case 6–2).

- The political system's memory is sometimes short, relying primarily on current or very recent results. A manager's distant

CASE
6–3

A DIPLOMATIC BLUNDER

Will Chester thinks the problem with his company's promotion system is that so much rides on the top man's judgment, which is based on brief encounters with employees. He wrote: "Back in 1976 I had the president visit my plant. We knew a day ahead of time, so my supervisors put in extra help the night before to make the production lines look a bit better. There were four extra cleanup night people. Well, it looked great. When the president and I walked the lines, he asked if it always looked this good. Here's where I called it as it was. I told him that I wished it could look this way, but trying to keep within our budget made it impossible to have conditions like this every day, and that we put on four extra night people because he was coming. You never know when some little thing like that gets blown out of all porportion."

CASE
6–4

A TOKEN WOMAN?

They offered me a shot at a management job, which was flattering to a woman. But I remember clearly sitting alone in the crowded cafeteria thinking it over. I looked around me at the sea of dark suits, white shirts, and black ties, and all these men became dummies to me—no feelings, no movements, just doll-like dummies. I was absolutely scared. I was becoming like them and destined ultimately to be a female token dummy. The flash was: in no way was I going to pay the price of my personhood to move up their ladder.

---

past successes or those in another location are forgotten. This short memory span cannot be functional (Case 6–3).

- The political system often is operated by a self-perpetuating ingroup, indifferent to the track records of managers.

The political system therefore may be necessary, but it is unjust if we believe good performance should be rewarded by promotion. Its standards are slippery, and its evidence is hearsay from faceless witnesses. Reputations are built according to what "they" say. The system flourishes through an old-boy network. In a simpler business world or with uncomplicated technology, old-boy impressionistic judgments of people might have been sufficient. But it is doubtful that this was ever true in the past, and it is a certain liability in the present corporation.

BUREAUCRACY

The bureaucratic system imposes standardized, impersonal, and objective decision making that follows stated rules and visible criteria. On the surface it would seem to be founded on two undoubted truths. First, the political system generates abuses of power and elevates some incompetent persons. Second, corporate organizations require some consistency in their methods for making decisions. Bureaucracy therefore reforms the abuses of the more informal political system by substituting orderly processes; especially, it substitutes quantitative ratings of performance. These ratings become a matter of record which can be consulted when we want to promote people of merit. Some efficiency is possible because ratings or numbers can be presented to boards and committees in color-coded form. The senior author remembers particularly the "war room" on which a large corporate office spent $250,000. Mounted in the room were projectors which could, on a 5-second notice, show the job, pay, and rating history of any of 4000 managers or engineers. The bureaucratic system brings deliberations into the open, thus eliminating the worst of backroom politics. However, it has unfortunate drawbacks:

- As noted in Chapter 4, even a casual glance at a bureaucratic rating sheet shows that few of the things rated are closely related to the organization's purpose in having the particular job done.

- Since employees and managers know these ratings are irrelevant, they do not take the trouble to make them seriously and, when the chips are down in a specific promotion decision, would prefer to disregard them.

- Managers try to give everyone good ratings, further weakening their meaning.

In brief, standardized, orderly, quantified junk *remains* junk. Lacking meaning, the bureaucratic procedures are reintegrated in the political system. Ratings are thus made to serve other purposes such as preserving goodwill or promoting favorites (Case 6–4).

TRAIT RATINGS

To escape irrelevant bureaucratic ratings, the system of trait ratings promotes candidates who can show the most impressive personal qualities. These qualities can be judged through personal interviews, testing, performance reviews, or assessment centers. The argument seems impressive: identify "qualified" people, and promote the ablest. This approach assumes that it is possible to determine traits with objectivity or without influence from the rater's own theories. While many of the procedures described produce ratings that will predict performance, serious scientific doubts persist about what is being rated. Ratings have often been shown to demonstrate more about the rater than about the person rated. In spite of the occasional validity studies reported, trait ratings remain under a cloud. We believe, however, that this cloud will dissipate when traits are defined with reference to track records rather than apart from them. In other words, why not judge human competence and motivation from well-documented track records?

BEHAVIORAL STANDARDS

As a sort of last gasp, traditional psychology devised a method called "behavioral standards." It advanced a well-reasoned argument, based on research, that traits cannot and should not be rated but that an employee's behavior can and should be rated. The method appeals for objectivity in evaluating a person for what he or she does rather than for hypothetical inner qualities. Behavioral standards overcome the irrelevance of bureaucratic evaluation by the choice of specific functional requirements such as coming to work on time, getting reports in, or making a certain number of sales calls. Moreover, the standards seem eminently fair because a person can know in advance what must be done to obtain a favorable rating. Such standards are, however, a false solution to the problem of judging the causes of results:

- An employee could comply with all the behavioral standards and be given a favorable rating for compliance while failing to produce the results which are the purpose of the job.

- Attention is distracted from the nature and goals of the job because in practice behavioral standards are difficult to set and are quite time-consuming.

- In particular, it is almost impossible to set relevant behavioral standards for higher levels of management.

THE TRACK RECORD AS A PRACTICAL OPTION

The power of tradition and other appeals of the competing systems described above are too great to hope to install a track record system as an alternative to them except in a newly formed corporation. Why not include their best qualities in a new system? After all, there are arguments for each of these systems. Since political influence is essential for success in an organization, a person's track record in influencing others may surely be considered. The orderliness of a commonly understood bureaucratic procedure can become an asset of a properly designed track record system. As to the inclusion of traits, since a trait fundamentally is consistency in a person, there is no real way to design a system totally without them. Last, certain requirements of prudent conduct would seem worth setting and including in the system, provided they do not dominate and distract us from the evaluation of working results.

Have we been saying that the virtues of competing systems may be retained while getting rid of their vices? We maintain guarded optimism that this can be done, provided the central element is performance.

PROPER LENGTH OF THE TRACK RECORD

To determine the causes of events, managers must furnish a sophisticated narrative history. We shall find that while this task sounds demanding, it actually need not cover one's entire life. Instead, it can be just long enough to cover the following necessary variations:

- It should include performance under more than one boss. Otherwise it is difficult to know how an individual performed under both favorable and unfavorable conditions.

- For the same reason, it should cover both prosperous and difficult economic times. The performance of others in the same area or in the same industry in the same period should be available for comparison.

- It should cover more than one job to make sure successes were not due to easy assignments and failures to impossible ones.

In theory, these variations can be met in as brief a period as 2 years. It is unlikely, however, that 2 years will provide enough contrast. In practice, many more years are required. We usually ask for results in working with the best boss one has ever had and also the worst, the easiest job and the hardest, in more than one company or location. These variations are often provided by a consistent running record covering about 6 years. Why not the entire work history? Some kind of statute of limitations should perhaps be imposed. We should judge the person as he or she is today. People should be permitted to change. Early failures should not be hung around a person's neck like an albatross forever. Nevertheless, an individual who shows conspicuous achievement at an early age, which is true in many creative pursuits, should be permitted to

POINTS OF VERIFIABILITY

A general manager wrote a series of critical incidents about his performance during the year 1968. He was reminded that in this system we verify claims. In the excerpt following, the points which we normally would verify (and did in this case) are underlined. He wrote: "Summary 1968—our customer contracted for eight large vessels. Part of the deal was to have propulsion built by Europeans. Specifically, the Belgians were to build turbines and gears for all ships. We had never been able to effect a satisfactory joint manufacturing agreement with that country regarding gears. I went to Belgium and with the customer's support was able for the first time to conclude a satisfactory arrangement with the Belgians to collaborate. This was a real breakthrough and led to overall agreement for future ships. The results were possible because of meticulous planning and development of what-if scenarios so that we were able to anticipate every move, objection, etc., and successfully counter it." (Underlining was made by an investigator who wanted to verify the account.)

produce it in evidence. Perhaps the positive statute of limitations should be much longer than the negative.

PREPARING THE TRACK RECORD

The only qualified observer, continuously present, is the performer. It is upon the performer that the main burden of preparation should be placed. It is true that the performer is a biased witness. Nevertheless, there is much that can be done to improve the objective content of the track record account. Objectivity is provided by the following:

- Ask the individual to include hard facts, where available, about both claimed successes and failures.
- Make sure he or she knows that the record will be verified at factual places (Case 6–5).

A CONFIRMABLE ACCOUNT

In Minnesota in 1961, a divorcee and an ex-convict were applying for employment. As personnel director, I knew that the general manager had personal scruples typical of a hypocritical religious environment. After satisfying myself about the qualifications and motivations of these persons, I undertook a personal selling job with the general manager, and he hired the divorcee as his secretary. The reformed convict was placed with the owner of a new supermarket as his general store manager. Both placements were highly successful for all parties. They were personal salvations for two employees who were fighting a previously losing battle in a hypocritical environment.

- Cross-examine the individual to minimize inevitable self-justification.

- Make a genuine effort to ensure that the performer knows that his or her best performance is the principal focus on the record while acknowledging the values shown by defeat.

- Chief among these values are what they show about courage, performance under fire, endurance under travail, and, in brief, the person's *hard values,* those shown in a time of testing. Only hard values are ultimately believable. We express this view by saying that we believe what the manager does when the chips are down. One way of obtaining this information is to ask the person what he or she has ever fought *for.* While the individual prepares the track record, others independently confirm its factual elements (Case 6–6). See also Table 6–1 below.

There is no one way to obtain a track record. The principal varieties in use include both oral and written records. Written accounts have been described in Chapter 2. The individual is given a free opportunity to present a narrative but is encouraged to be specific. A narrative is, of course, a natural story. It is the way we talk about our work over a drink with the inevitable mixture of self-justification, strong feelings, and facts. It is usually easier to dis-

TABLE
6–1

FIELD-FORCE ANALYSIS OF CRITICAL INCIDENT IN CASE 6–6

Supports	Hindrances
1. Good relationship with the boss and with the supermarket personnel department	1. Hypocritical religious environment favoring punishing women for divorce
2. Top qualifications and motivation on the part of the two candidates	2. Recent publicity proving that you can't rehabilitate most ex-convicts
3. Growing climate of support both for equal opportunity and for helping to rehabilitate criminals	3. Doubts about whether the personnel director was a "bleeding heart" liberal who did not have the company's interests at heart
4. Personnel shortages at the time	

count self-justification later if the individual is permitted to offer it early. "Get it off your chest" is a good rule in preparing at least early drafts of a performance history.

The oral history is a presentation, usually to members of a panel who will judge promotion fitness. It is falsely felt that the wisdom of such panels, which are often used in government and in upper-management circles in industry, exempts the members from requiring evidence for their decisions. Since the future of a business depends on the validity of panel judgments, one would suppose ground rules, disciplined operation, and training would be required of panels. Such a policy lies in the future. Panels are often politically chosen; they feel above reflections on their judgments and function much like juries.

One thing that has been done is to prepare candidates for meeting such panels so that they are on a more nearly equal footing. One company encouraged thirty upper-level managers to spend 2 days reviewing their track records in detail. When they boiled these track records down to what they each actually demonstrated about the managers' competence and values, the managers were able to make very assertive brief statements, well founded on the facts of their track records. This put them in a strong position in presenting themselves to the company's upper-level panels of executives.

JUDGING THE ACCOUNT

What a panel does in reviewing a written or fully presented oral account is a matter of its own logic and rigor of thought. Here, however, are a few suggestions. First, the panel should judge the account at the "business end" before proceeding to consider what the account proves. By the business end, we mean tangible results which are largely beyond dispute. Business results are of a limited number of types: financial, sales, or other essentially external results in a business's environment which affect its survival and growth. Many executives who judge managers believe the track record speaks for itself. It does not. As remarked earlier, no financial result can possibly evaluate itself. It must be evaluated in the context of the period in which it was achieved, the cost of the result, and whether the manager reporting the result actually produced it. The result may have been an accident, it may have been produced by the efforts of others, or, as sometimes happens, it may have been an unwise or ill-timed success. The panel must judge these things and not let the business results do their thinking for them.

A manager should be judged for all his or her results rather than piecemeal. That is, a person's results are the total output of his or her position. Results are often interrelated, one good result being achieved at the expense of another. Sophisticated evaluation involves an appreciation of this interconnection of results within the context of the environment in which they were produced or failed to be produced.

Next, the panel should characterize the environment, which is everything external to the individual that supported or entered

TABLE

6–2

FIELD-FORCE ANALYSIS OF A CONSTRUCTION COMPANY
MANAGER'S ANNUAL REPORT REGARDING THE YEAR WHEN
HE DID NOT MEET HIS EXPANSION OBJECTIVES

Supports	Hindrances
1. The new corporate president was strongly expansionist.	1. The company did not accept my budgetary recommendations.
2. There were strong subordinates; the top staff did a great job.	2. The government interfered with rezoning in our largest metropolitan program.
	3. There was growing uncertainty in the union-management climate in the Eastern provinces.
	4. Inflation increased by 2 percent over expectations, increasing our costs, which we could not absorb because of our long-term contracts.

those results. Table 6–2 shows a typical field-force analysis of one
manager's results. The manager can control some parts of the environment, and his coping with these parts becomes a portion of the
evaluation. However, the manager cannot control other parts of the
environment, such as a budget which he did not decide, and this
fact should be considered in determining his degree of responsibility for the results.

Finally, after the results and the environment have been clarified, we are in a position to judge the manager's utilization of
resources, which include time, money, and personnel, among other
factors. What we rate is the degree to which the person used avail-

able resources and whether utilization was commensurate with the results obtained. The account must therefore include a statement of the resources available to the manager.

Much has been omitted from the above analysis. What, for example, about the manager's traits or style of operation? We believe that this is too subtle a question to be put to promotion panels. A panel that evaluates the extent to which the manager has produced good results and shown sterling qualities in times of trouble has all it can do without considering psychological subtleties. What has already been said is subtle enough. While we are in doubt about promotion panels as they now are constituted, it is possible that research will prove that we were too pessimistic. There are these possibilities:

1. Research may show that panels can judge action qualities such as those described in earlier chapters of this book.

2. Research may discover ways of identifying circular programs in a manager's performance.

The term "circular program" refers to repetitive cycles of events within a manager's career which show capacity to accomplish self-defeat brilliantly or seemingly to rescue defeat from the jaws of victory. In theory, the circular program explains why so many promising individuals fail to use undoubted potential. We are not convinced that promotion panels *can* judge such subtleties. We are convinced that they can and must learn to dig into performance accounts to know who is accountable for good or poor results and to adjust the organization's reward system accordingly.

ACTION SUGGESTIONS

You had better be willing to do something about promotions. Your company or division has a short future if you are not promoting performers. Here are some options—things to check, actions to take:

- *Find out how political your system really is.* One test: does each person at the top have a favorite candidate and is willing to make selection a personal issue when it's time to promote? Sizing up the politics of your system merits a carefully designed survey.

- *Is the bureaucratic procedure for promotion choking off your top candidates?* How many persons who are actually top performers are getting average ratings?

- *Investigate men of distinction.* Use the chart in Table 5–1 in Chapter 5 to check how many recently promoted people have greater social than performance merit.

- *Consider good conduct.* Do boy scouts get promoted faster than top performers? (We are talking not about ethics but about conformity to rules versus showing results.)

- *Do something.* A step-by-step plan is shown earlier in this chapter under "Track Record Promotion." If you don't like the above findings, start taking these steps.

7

HIRE FOR THE
TRACK RECORD

Few managers realize that the hiring interview is in serious trouble. It's in serious trouble because research shows that the way in which it is ordinarily conducted doesn't produce valid conclusions. This is a business problem, an economic problem, and, in equal-opportunity situations, a legal problem. In this chapter we propose a solution that retains the interview as one of the most valuable organized business conversations that you can hold, but we propose to structure it more fully—fully enough to make it evidentiary, that is, to produce job-relevant information, but not to the extent that it spoils the creativity of both the interviewer and the applicant. The second feature in what we call the "track record interview" is that the interview is based on the rights of both parties: that of the *applicant* to describe his or her qualifications in his or her own way and that of the *company* to evaluate that evidence.

THE BUSINESS OPPORTUNITY

The interview is often taken for granted. Since it is an "organized conversation having a business purpose," as one authority has put it, seasoned managers consider that they already know how to conduct it. Others recognize that there is a bit more to interviewing than natural conversation and want training for themselves or, if they delegate interviewing, for others. No matter how well the training is carried out, however, the traditional hiring interview is in serious trouble, and other forms of organized conversation are available and should be sought. As these forms represent new directions, a good case for innovation needs to be made.

Among all the decisions about personnel, the hiring decision is the easiest to analyze economically, at least in principle. For some reason, managers who count their pennies on everything else in business find it not quite relevant to count them on personnel decisions. This cannot be a wise omission, since payroll is the largest cost you likely have. Without any pretense at a formula, we suggest that you consider the costs incurred from turnover and replacement. If you do a careful enough analysis and have never done one before, you are in for a shock. Replacement costs, including the time of supervisors to get new employees up to speed, interviewing finalists, screening candidates, recruiting, and paying tax and insurance penalties for the turnover, all these enter in. An automobile company estimated that it costs $50,000, in 1970 dollars, to replace a first-echelon foreman. Insurance companies have stated a cost of $20,000 for a sales representative. A sizable proportion of the first year's salary would be a rough rule of thumb (*you* decide on the proportion).

A $50,000 decision, the risk if you are wrong in your choice, deserves more than the 5 minutes it got according to one study of the time interviewers take for the decision. It is hard to justify a 5-minute interview; in the study what actually happened was that interviewers spent 1 hour but made the decision in the first 5 minutes. No doubt you are more thoughtful than that.

If you hire a number of persons each year, you can calculate the value of the hour against the savings achieved by making better decisions. Suppose that you are hiring sales representatives with a turnover cost of $20,000 and that you pick 20 a year. The cost of $400,000 can never be totally eliminated: you will never reach the point of perfect choices. But if you improve your selection judgment by, say, 20 percent, you will save $80,000. This means doing a better job of whatever the number of hours you spend picking 20.

Hours will range from 4 per job (say, for interviewing 4 finalists in 1 hour each for each job) on up. If a conservative figure of 80 hours (4 hours for 20 jobs) is used and you succeed in saving $80,000, your interviewing time begins to look worth more than you thought. How many ways are there for you to make $1000 an hour for yourself or your company?

THE TRACK RECORD INTERVIEW

The track record interview (TRI) is based on principles developed in Chapter 6 but applied to the particular case in which there is a face-to-face interview. This interview is a time-honored tradition in hiring, but as we shall find, it is a very expensive tradition without modification. By using the track record interview, we believe that you can drastically reduce testing and save expensive assessment centers for selection in critical situations in which the centers' value has the greatest payoff. You can also achieve better integration of two hiring needs: to conduct a professional interview and to involve the future supervisor in the final job offer. The track record interview, if recorded (Table 7-1), is more efficient because it permits a person to tell his or her story once but may be replayed as often as necessary to get a reliable evaluation. This system contrasts with the traditional interview, in which an individual may be asked to tell his or her story to several persons. But the major advantage of the track record interview is to obtain in a fairly short time substantial job-relevant evidence to provide a basis for hiring as opposed to the intuitive impressions of interviewers.

How It Works

The track record interview is an organized conversation in which the applicant is told enough about the job to be able to present reasons for confidence that he or she can handle it. The candidate is then permitted to amplify these reasons to the satisfaction of the interviewer so that their factual basis can be established. Finally, the interviewer evaluates this *evidence* rather than personal impres-

TABLE
7-1

RECORDING FORM FOR TRACK RECORD INTERVIEW

Job Element A	Job Element B	Job Element C	Job Element D	Job Element E
Under each job element write one or two sentences summarizing the key aspects of the element as you want the candidate to understand it. It is not necessary to write a complete job description.				
In this part of each column, write a few notes on the reasons the candidate offers for being qualified to carry out the job element of that column. These notes are cues for what to expand later in the inquiry.				
In this part of each column, write a few notes to summarize how likely it is that the candidate can get up to speed on the job quickly. These might be things which appear difficult or about which the candidate would like to know more. Or they might be areas in which the candidate wonders if you have training. Or add other questions of your own.				
Rating of A:———	Rating of B:———	Rating of C:———	Rating of D:———	Rating of E:———

sions of the candidate. The effect is to place the burden of data production on the candidate and the burden of evaluation on the interviewer. We consider this a more proper division of labor in recognizing the rights of both candidate and company. Such an interview produces the kinds of accounts defined in earlier chapters, especially critical incidents and annual reports, because these kinds of data have a high proportion of verifiable statements. The pressure is put on the candidate to be honest. The reliability and validity of the interview have a chance to be high.

Principles Involved in Track Record Interviewing

Among the principles involved in the proper design of such an interview, the following should be mentioned:

- The track record principle: a person can do again what he or she has done in the past.

- Job relevance refers to the capacity of the track record to indicate the candidate's chances to do well on this job and in this work setting.

- Evidence consists of whatever facts or information about the track record are found to be job-relevant.

Steps in the Interview

In general, the interviewer obtains data in the form shown in Table 7-1. Notice that the columns in the form represent the elements of the job to be filled. There are two parts of each column. Above the second line we consider the evidence which supports the candidacy, and below the line the arguments against the candidacy. The problem of the interview's design is how to obtain these two kinds of information. On the positive, upper side of the line, the candidate is permitted to present any information he or she wants. The interviewer later returns to amplify the information and judge its relevance. Below the second line the problem changes. We shall not ask a candidate to testify against himself or herself. Another kind of question is more reasonable (the intent is not to ask a trick question); that is, we ask the candidate to volunteer correctable shortfalls in performance. (A correctable shortfall is a limitation which a candidate thinks can be overcome in time.) We ask the candidate to tell us about these shortfalls to help us evaluate his or her candidacy. Our experience is that candidates, unless they are suspicious, are willing to do this once its relevance has been explained.

1. First, we say to the candidate, "Let me outline to you what this job is—its several elements. Then see how you fit. I want you to tell me why you think you can do the thing described in this element. That is, you have some reason for believing yourself qualified to do it." The interviewer explains the job element and, if the candidate has no questions, goes on to the next job element with the same presentation. The interviewer continues until the major parts of the job have been described. If the candidate understands what has been said, he or she should be able to give reasons for thinking he or she can handle the job. Otherwise, why apply?

2. The interviewer may now say something like, "Now if all this is clear, tell me why you think you can do this [first job element]." The interviewer makes a few notes, a phrase or so to which the interviewer will later return for amplification. In Table 7–2 we show a sample set of interview notes. After getting notes on the first job element, the interviewer goes on to the next one, and so on, until he has made whatever notes are desired above the second line. The process is made visible: it is important that the interviewer explain to the person how he or she is proceeding. Cards are not held close to the vest. The effect on the candidate is to create a good atmosphere for the next step.

3. The interviewer now is ready to develop some initial ideas below the second line. The interviewer may say, "To get an idea of how fast you can fit into this job means to find out what special support you'll need to get up to speed. So I'm going to make some notes below the line here about things that trouble you about this job element. This will tell me what you'll need from me or from others to get yourself up to what you consider your own standard of performance." Most people will volunteer some limitations or

concerns; others will be wary. There is no way, of course, to compel disclosure of this kind of information.

4. The interviewer now is ready to go back and amplify. This means to single out key facts in each column and find out what they mean. For example, if the person says, "I handled this product line for 3 years," the question becomes, "How well did you do and under what conditions? In what kind of territory?" In general, facts do not speak for themselves but make sense to the interviewer only when put in context and amplified with details. If the person says, "I possess Quality X [such as a trait], which makes me feel that I can do this job element well," the interviewer may say, "Give me an example of that quality, so I see what you mean." The candidate should describe examples of on-the-job demonstration of the quality rather than paraphrasing it and defining what was meant by the quality.

5. After amplifying all the major facts considered relevant, the interviewer may turn to the résumé or application blank and clear up any troubling questions about voids, confusing information, or neglected areas in the person's background. We will not try to discuss this kind of questioning, but all managers know that it is governed increasingly by legal considerations in equal-opportunity cases.

6. The TRI has ended, and the manager now "scores" the evidence. In each column consider which of the facts that the interviewer regards as credible and relevant should be given most weight. In effect, these are gold stars. An ideal candidate would have a gold star in his or her column. Other facts which support the candidacy and are credible and relevant, if not outstanding, are pluses. Minuses would be marked in each column according to facts which weaken the candidacy or show high requirements in terms of training time required to get the candidate up to speed.

Decision Making

What about getting other people's opinions? In many companies, the practice of multiple interviewing is followed. While this may be

TABLE
7-2

SAMPLE INTERVIEWER NOTES

Job Element A	Job Element B	Job Element C	Job Element D	Job Element E
Improve communications between managers and engineers. Get data showing where these are most serious.	Facilitate growth in key managers. Assess needs for training and see that they are rotated frequently.	Call attention of managers to new developments in behavioral sciences which bear on our company.	Teach basic programs in management by objective. Candidate must be especially effective at the case method.	Build a more innovative program. Our training seminars have not significantly changed in 5 years. Candidate must sell skeptical engineers.
Candidate has not done this kind of work before. Believes could do it but has not given any reason for optimism.	In previous company, many of the 100 key managers he worked with got promoted. Was given considerable credit.	For the last 2 years wrote a quarterly newsletter.	Can show "rave ratings" from managers who went through his seminars.	Believes newsletter was innovative. Reluctant to offer suggestions until he sees some of the seminars and outlines.
Would like to get some training in industrial relations.	None.	None.	None.	Personal selling experience weak. Would like some instruction or direction in how to improve.

essential to learn whether the candidate mixes well with others, it should not provide the main line of evidence on which hiring decisions are made. Instead, the manager may record the track record interview and have it heard and rated independently by others. This does not mean that the candidate might not briefly meet others, provided intuitive impressions are not used as a substitute for genuine evidence.

How is the decision finally made? We shall not attempt to develop an elaborate point-scoring system here except to say that, in general, gold stars awarded for critical job elements indicate the likelihood that a candidate can do the work again. There must, however, be some relationship between the evidence recorded and the points awarded. The manager must be able to say where he or she got the reasons for awarding the points. As to whether some job elements should be given more points than others, in practice this kind of weighting has rarely proved worth the statistical trouble it takes. It would be better to be sure that the job elements listed include no trivia and to weight everything equally.

We have used a number of terms in the brief description of the interview above. Here is what these terms mean:

- *Track record.* The long-term record of factual accomplishments in similar work.

- *Credentials.* Factual accomplishments, results, recognition, or certification not in similar work. Credentials might include a college degree, a patent, or club memberships. An important limitation of credentials is that they indicate past opportunities better than they indicate ability to produce working results.

- *Evidence.* Any result, especially a work sample, fully enough described to show its job relevance, its verifiability, and the person's actual accountability in producing the result.

- *Amplification.* Interviewer's questions aimed at getting a person to expand on a claimed qualification in order to make the claim evidentiary.

- *Consolidation.* Questions aimed at making the claims of the candidate more clear, precise, and verifiable.

- *Personality questions.* Questions aimed at finding out what the person is like rather than what the person can do or has done. Don't ask such questions.

- *Prejudicial questions.* Questions which make it hard for the person to present evidence on his or her behalf.

- *Prejudice.* Scoring anything not evidentiary in order to exclude a person from an opportunity for demographic reasons (age, sex, race, etc.).

- *Track record assessment.* Finding out what past results may be attributed to a candidate to forecast future performance.

- *Track record interview.* Conducting a track record assessment by means of conversation.

PROS AND CONS

You may ask whether we should interview at all. There is abundant evidence that interviewers perceive candidates in a trivial fashion (making a major decision on the basis of a 2- or 3-minute interview, for example), are unreliable and biased, and do not reach valid conclusions. Does this not argue for more objective methods such as testing or for more observational (and less wordy) methods such as assessment centers? Have we not especially weakened our position by permitting the most biased witness of all, the candidate for the job, to take the stand? Another objection is that the interview, since it allows a person to appear in the flesh, evokes the many prejudices interviewers have about appearance. Why not use simple paper procedures without the appearance of the candidate? A special argument against the track record interview is that it is very simple. Few if any standardized questions are used. How can anything this simple be as effective as testing or assessment centers? A final general objection is the danger that a candidate lacking verbal skills could not receive an equal opportunity to be considered for a job.

COMPARISON WITH TRADITIONAL INTERVIEWING

There are some similarities and contrasts in the two types of interviews. Both consist of conversational self-presentation. One difference is that the TRI is more generally structured around the job, the column headings (Table 7-1) differing with each job. The traditional interview focused on the person, whereas the newer interviewing focuses on the history relevant to the particular job. The traditional interviewer made an evaluation as the interview proceeded. In the TRI, an evaluation is made only after all the evidence is in. The traditional interviewer's bias was uncontrollable, in part because of the vague qualities that often were rated. In the new interview, bias is controllable because *evidence,* not a person, is evaluated. Top traditional interviewers probably are rare. The TRI is easier to learn. Finally, authoritarian methods could be used in traditional interviewing, in the sense that the interviewer took the lead and the applicant supplied answers. The process was much like an examination. The TRI emphatically is not a form of examination: it is an opportunity to present oneself, and it assumes that the candidate has an adult's mastery of his or her qualifications.

In general, the new interview has the following advantages over the old one:

- It places a greater burden on the candidate.

- It removes some mysteries by making the structure of the interview visible and describing the job as completely as the candidate wishes.

- No traits are rated.

- Appearance and manner are not rated unless they are a clear job requirement.

- The evidence is not lost but can be recorded and rerated by others.

- The TRI is job-relevant in its very structure.

- Accounts of the past are at least as verifiable as the impressions obtained by traditional interviewing, and probably are more verifiable.

The Future of Interviewing

Should we interview at all, since there are so many problems? Managers insist on seeing people before job offers are made. True, persons who show up in their best clothes may not always look and sound as they do when "up" for an interview. While direct impressions may be misleading, however, people in business are not going to do without them. There is a second reason for insisting on an interview: fairness. It seems markedly unfair to make a decision vital to a person's future without a chance for the person to influence it. The interview provides a chance to make a self-presentation. Although many find this chance anxiety-provoking, they would feel a sense of acute grievance if they were denied it. Third, new departures in structured interviewing hold out the chance that, given proper training, interviewers collecting evidence rather than impressions may well turn out to be valid decision makers.

THE ASSESSMENT CENTER

Having disposed, we hope, of the traditional interview, we shall turn to newer alternatives. The "assessment center" is the newest invention in personnel selection and has enjoyed rapid and well-deserved growth in the United States and other industrial countries. In this approach to selection, the candidate is given tasks simulating what a person would have to do on the job if hired. A qualified observer rates the candidate's performance on the task. Most such tasks are done in a group, with several observers rating the performance. To managers who think every selection method is a test, the novelty of the assessment center may not be clear. The center mostly uses simulation of work and rarely any paper-and-pencil tests. For example, in the original assessment centers (those of the Office of Strategic Services in World War II), potential agents were appraised under stress or in tasks such as moving across unfamiliar country at night (this is a far cry from paper-and-pencil tests). Cross-country hiking would be simulation if that is what agents do.

Like the TRI, the assessment center focuses on job-relevant performance. In both systems, a panel of raters can be used, and the raters must be trained. Often line managers who know the job best are employed as raters.

The two systems differ, however, in important respects. While the center provides live observation, the TRI obtains data referring to the past. The evaluation made at the conclusion of the center's program produces trait ratings, whereas the evaluation made from the TRI evidence consists of estimates of how well the candidate would handle the job. Both kinds of selection require training, but assessment-center training seems rather lengthy, whereas fairly short training is sufficient for the TRI. The center provides direct observation in an artificial environment, while track record interviewing obtains accounts of actual performance in a real environment.

There are additional advantages to the assessment center. One is the involvement of line managers in a project which several can do together. The standardized exercises they use have many of the advantages of traditional testing as well as a live-action quality. It is that quality which gives the center its principal advantage: credibility. Finally, the assessment center is not so verbal as a track record interview.

The advantages of the track record interview over the assessment center are:

- Evidence drawn from longer periods
- Performance in real, not artificial, environments
- A chance to speak for oneself
- Briefer training for the interviewer

- No evaluation of traits

- The fact that data obtained in track record interviews are criterion data (properly recorded performance accounts are the bottom line of management)

- The possibility of a recorded TRI's being rerated as many times as necessary for scientific or legal reasons

In summary, the assessment center has important advantages over the TRI, but its limitations are sufficient to require, in our judgment, that structured interviews such as the TRI be used as the major form of selection in hiring situations.

TESTS AND COMPETENCY MEASURES

By tests, we mean paper-and-pencil tests of ability, interest, and knowledge. These may be called competency measures if they are obviously relevant to the job. For example, mathematical tests may be given to sales candidates. They become competency measures if they are composed of problems actually faced by sales representatives on the job to be filled. Thus, tests can be made job-relevant as in the TRI. Like the TRI, tests give the person a chance to show what he or she can do. Finally, tests and competency measures obtain explicit evidence which many persons can review and evaluate against the job's requirements.

Tests have certain advantages over the TRI:

- They are objective in both administration and interpretation.

- They are simpler and easier to research than the TRI.

- They require less time from management.

- They do not use a biased witness.

The advantages of the TRI over tests are:

- It allows the person to speak on his or her own behalf, an elementary right that is neglected if testing alone is used.

- It is more human and personal, providing an opportunity to interact.

- Since tests must ultimately be evaluated against the kind of evidence collected in the TRI (namely, track record evidence), why not collect this kind of evidence in the first place?

- There is greater dignity for the candidate in the track record interview. He or she is given the compliment of being allowed to volunteer reasons for expecting success if hired. In contrast, the person being tested is called a "subject" and often feels in a passive student's role, as in earlier life when a test was given by a teacher.

HOW TO SET UP A TRACK RECORD INTERVIEWING SYSTEM

The TRI can be no better than the job analysis on which it is based. Therefore, if there's a question about the precise content of the job to be filled, this must be studied before setting up a TRI system. The same is true of any other hiring procedure. For a job analysis, the critical-incident approach is the closest to reality. The management of a pharmaceutical company that desired to upgrade interviewing began with just such an approach. Twenty-five sales representatives were questioned, and about 100 critical incidents of effective and ineffective sales performance were collected by the interviewers. These were analyzed to determine the job elements of the position. It is that analysis which provides the structure for the TRI. In collecting such information as critical incidents, we assume that management must specify the results desired on a job, but only the best workers can ordinarily describe the actions which are effective in getting these results. Thus, while critical incidents were obtained from the pharmaceutical sales representatives to describe how they obtained or missed sales, it was the managers who rated the results in the incidents. The result was a list of action qualities rather than duties.

One day of training for seasoned managers is ordinarily suffi-

TABLE
7-3

OUTLINE OF SEMINAR IN DEVELOPING ABILITY TO HANDLE A TRACK RECORD INQUIRY

9:00 A.M.   Orientation to modern techniques in recruiting, selecting, and orienting new employees. Legal aspects. Scientific aspects. Ethics: what you owe the applicant and the company.

9:30 A.M.   Building a job profile to guide selection.

9:45 A.M.   Using the application blank to pinpoint areas where the interviewer should raise questions.

10:15 A.M.   Sample traditional interview; color videotape of a short interview.

10:30 A.M.   Critique of traditional interview: why ratings cannot be traced back to solid evidence in the interview.

11:00 A.M.   Second videotape, "modeling" a track record inquiry.

11:30 A.M.   Structure of the track record inquiry: job relevance; self-advocacy evidence; steps in conducting an inquiry.

1:00 P.M.   Laboratory practice in trios. Each "applies" for a job and is given a track record inquiry. The second person interviews. The third person observes and gives critique.

2:00 P.M.   Rotate roles.

3:15 P.M.   Rotate roles.

4:15 P.M.   Discuss plans to apply the method.

5:00 P.M.   Certification and wrap-up.

cient to orient them to track record interviewing. The key points to which managers must assent if the system is to work are:

- It will cost them dearly if they neglect evidence in hiring.

- Evidence can be obtained, and they do not need to rely on gut feeling, as in the past.

- This kind of interviewing is an interesting experience for candidates, an excellent way either to launch a person's tenure with the company or to obtain the respect of unsuccessful candidates.

- A sample training outline, developed at the Pepsi-Cola Company, is shown in Table 7-3.

After this training, managers should be ready to use track record interviewing procedures.

OTHER KINDS OF STRUCTURED INTERVIEW

The track record interview is described in this chapter because it uses the concepts presented in earlier chapters of the book. However, this interview is one of many varieties of "patterned interview."

The difference between a patterned and a more traditional interview is that the former has an explicit strategy. The strategy of the track record interview is to get the candidate to volunteer relevant working accounts from the past. Any patterned interview has a strategy. Another (not recommended) would be to place stress on the candidate, on the theory that the person with the thickest skin would do best.

What is *said* in the patterned interview (its tactics) depends on that strategy. Is it possible to prescribe what is said so fully that the interviewer knows, at every step, what to say next? This method would provide tactics without a flexible strategy and deprive the interviewer of scope for creativity and improvisation. Such a procedure is no longer an interview but is better called interrogation or even testing.

The loss of intelligence in such an interviewer is similar to that of a man who did not have the interviewer's flexibility of varying his questions. Instead, he interrogated his dinner partner, whom he had just met, by asking, "Are you married?" When she answered, "No," he asked the next question in his prescribed routine, "Do you have children?" Whereupon she clubbed him. He then turned to his partner on the other side, with a second routine, held in readiness if the first interrogation should fail to thaw someone, asking, "Do you have children?" When she answered "Yes," he then asked the next question in this routine, "Are you married?" Whereupon, etc.

ACTION SUGGESTIONS

The traditional impressionistic interview presents serious scientific and legal problems. The temptation is to send your people or yourself to one of the well-organized interviewer-training programs commonly available.

Don't

Do not embark on such a program unless the trainer can show you how the interview design overcomes the weaknesses of impressionistic interviewing. That is, the trainer ought to know about the weaknesses which have been demonstrated in research. These include:

- Bias.

- Limited attention span of interviewers. They typically stop after hearing one negative fact from an applicant.

- Excessive concern with how well the two people relate rather than with whether any real evidence for job potential is resulting.

Do

- Talk to your attorney. Don't let him or her off the hook by merely telling you which questions are illegal. Find out the latest precedents on the interview.

- Set up a track record interviewing system. Follow the program outlined in this chapter.

TRANSCRIPT OF A TRACK RECORD INQUIRY

LEN: You're Bill Jones? Welcome. . . . I guess you are interested in the job with engineering?

BILL: That's the one—I've been in manager development work [at Sonnenberg] with sales people and manufacturing, but never engineering.

LEN: Your credentials looked right to me the other day, so I thought we'd talk. Let me cover the job briefly, and then you tell me how it fits what you've done.

Basically we break down all jobs for talking purposes into five areas. Just a rule of thumb. This job has communications, counseling, education, training, and design functions.

By communications I mean between managers and engineers. We've had some turmoil. It's gotten up to the board, and they handed this little hot potato to our department. We want somebody to survey the situation—four management and two engineering groups—and pinpoint some issues we can surface and cope with. Any questions on what I'm driving at?

BILL: No.

LEN: Job Element B means to work with individual managers, get to 'em once every so often, talk about how well they are coming along, what our department needs to do. They don't always think about their own needs for training. We also can set up a job rotation. Any questions?

BILL: Sounds like the usual. Be interesting to rotate some engineers through the management jobs and vice versa.

LEN: You dreamer, you! Now Job Element C is a study job. Get up to speed on the behavioral sciences. Brief our managers on what is new that they ought to know. We make audiovisual equipment behaviorists use, I guess you know. But mainly, things like what NTL is doing that our managers might want to hear about. They're high on NTL here. Questions?

BILL: I'd be willing to do something like that on my own time.

LEN: Don't give anything away. Job Element D. That's your stand-up training. A little bit of everything but more of the Bus Ad programs than you might think. If you can teach labor, accounting, finance, production management, law, and international relations, you're in.

BILL: What?

LEN: I'm kidding. Not all that, but some. How are you on case method?

BILL: It's out of date to just do that. But it's bread-and-butter training; everyone has to do it.

LEN: Job Element E. We've let our complacency build up around here. No real changes in our basic training seminars in 5 years. Want somebody to shake it up with new ideas and then sell the engineers. I mean go out and get them to realize they are not feeding enough people through here. One-to-one selling on a personal basis. Questions?

BILL: No, but I've never done that. That is, no selling. Innovation in training, yes.

LEN: Do you have any questions on any of the five areas?

BILL: They sound clear to me, although it would take a while to know where the bodies are buried around here.

LEN: Well, now I want to shift gears and go into your qualifications. Start back at Area A—improve communications between managers and engineers. I'd like to know how effective you'd be and why you think so.

BILL: Really effective. That'd be the most interesting part of the job. I'd like to learn a lot more about industrial relations.

LEN: Yes, but I want to know *why* you think you'd be good at it. What have you ever done like it? If not, what makes you think you could do it?

BILL: I've never done anything just like that. But I'd like to try it.

LEN: Well on B, that's facilitating growth of individual managers.

BILL: How many would I see?

LEN: 200, mostly middle and a few upper.

BILL: Sonnenberg, I worked with 100 guys. Most of the ones up for promotion got a good rating on potential. It had something to do with my counseling. And out of that 100, 30 have actually been promoted in the 4 years I was there. You'll find—there are a couple of names it'd be all right to call there—I was well known as an aggressive developer.

LEN: That's interesting. When we are through, I'd like you to leave those names, and I'd like you to write me a memo on three examples of your work. I want to hear what was tough or easy about each of the people. And what happened that convinced you your work was successful. Now on Area C, you seemed to be quite interested in the behavioral sciences part of the job?

BILL: That is in line with my graduate study. I know I would do a good job on that because for the last two years I wrote a quarterly newsletter for managers. Abstracted some experiments or research which relates to some things the company is worried about. My stuff got read and it would be quoted in memos coming around. People dropped by and talked to me about things I wrote.

LEN: How much time did that take, and what did you invest in the newsletter?

BILL: I wrote it in 2 days each issue. In between issues, I systematically digested so many articles a week, kept a file.

LEN: I'd like to read the last four newsletters. Now I want to go into Areas D and E with you tomorrow since our time has run out.

BILL: Sorry you don't want to hear about D because I got my "rave ratings" from managers on that. Guys who went through my seminars.

LEN: Well, we are out of time.

BILL: And on E, you said you want a more innovative program. I want to bring you my newsletter tomorrow. It's full of ideas.

LEN: Well, like I said, we're out of time today. . . .

8

EXPERIENCE— A COMEBACK?

Most managers and all union leaders agree on one key way to value a person: for *experience.* The seasoned manager has had a chance to learn something; the senior worker, too. But managers and unions make up a minority. In the United States, at least, society has been youth-oriented for some decades. Sometimes the value placed on youth is practical: the new, younger worker supposedly costs less to hire. A policy of hiring the young is not always one of overvaluing them; rather, it is a policy of refusing to pay for the value of experience. However, genuine value is set upon youth in such diverse ways as:

- Idealizing youthful beauty
- Imitating the talk of the young
- Idolizing contact sports
- Featuring advertising copy with "now" people doing teen-age things
- Choosing immature people as celebrities

It is not only sports, looks, and style that are valued. So are youthful accomplishments. Lehman (1953) showed many years ago that in a wide range of fields the achievers' peak years, in which their accomplishments were most frequent, were their twenties. This was true in such fields as poetry, mathematics, science, and literature. The exceptions, fields in which frequency of achievement came late, were in problematic occupations and areas of accomplishment:

- Biology, psychology, and social science
- Philosophy
- Religious leadership
- Political leadership

These areas are problematic in the sense that their celebrities are not universally admired (the exception might be biology). Let us consider the others. Psychology, as a field, has gained rapidly increasing acceptance, but it cannot be said to have universal status, especially among politically and socially conservative people. Social science is controversial. Religious leaders have undergone a distinct decline in prestige. Need we comment on the prestige of politicians?

The consequences of our youth-oriented culture are not difficult to derive. Because age is undervalued, there are job difficulties: difficulties in relocating after 40, decreases in morale shown by high suicide rates after 60, and increases in alcoholism after 60. In short, according to many social indicators the lot of the aging in our culture is poor.

Before you say, "So the lot of the old is bad; that's nothing new," note the contradictions. Managers and unions believe that seniority or seasoning should have value, but it is not valued. If there is indeed something about experience that should be valued (and *is* valued according to most of the world's cultures), perhaps our values are distorted and will eventually return to "normal." We therefore expect a reappraisal in the future. There are, in fact, signs of change, if only in the form of increasing political power for older groups (Case 8–1).

AGE CLOUT

Margaret Kuhn, 72, "the charismatic founder of the Gray Panthers, a highly vocal movement of some 10,000 members is out to rid the country of 'age-ism,' —discrimination based on age." On mandatory retirement from the Presbyterian Church missions, she decided "the time was ripe for us to fight back." She has since been traveling some 100,000 miles a year, delivering at least 200 lectures and contributing all her fees to the Gray Panthers. Active picket and lobbyist in Washington, she is credited as having something to do with House and Senate formation of select committees on aging, and the presence of an adviser in the White House. Mandatory retirement age may be lifted to 70. The Gray Panthers also produce a newspaper, have radio programs, monitor the media for negative stereotyping of old people. She once appeared on Carson's Tonight show, where she says, "I told him his portrayal (of the crotchety Aunt Blabby) was unfair, unpleasant, and a whole lot of bull." However, Maggie points with approval to Carson's new policy of not dying his hair but letting it show gray. Ms. Kuhn speaks—and apparently acts—toward welding old and young people into a coalition for political change. She believes young and old should share housing. Her own Philadelphia home is shared with people aged 25, 30, and 35—plus Maggie Kuhn, 72. From George Michaelson, Maggie Kuhn: Gray Panther on the Prowl, *Parade*, Dec. 18, 1977, 7–8.

Our conclusion is that we are approaching a watershed in employment regarding age. There are options: the two largest are that either we will have a pressure-group philosophy (assertive advocacy of the rights of older employees) or our society will learn to identify and honor the assets of seasoned people.

This chapter pursues the second option. There is time to adopt it. It remains to be seen whether you will teach yourself to take a new look at mid-career employees, including yourself if you are of that vintage, or whether you will let pressure groups lead you into reforms.

The assumptions of this chapter are:

- If experience is indeed an asset, it should be valued and fully credited.

- To value experience cannot be to measure years spent doing something, although this measurement may well be part of our valuing procedure.

- Experience is too complex for a single valuing procedure.

A CASE FOR SENIORITY

However we may feel about seniority, let us first consider its claims as a measure of experience. This examination will teach us something of the meaning of experience as an asset. We can then see how to proceed, to improve upon seniority as a measure. The prerogative seniority rests upon number of years spent doing something, perhaps in a given location or as a member of a certain organization. This definition claims almost total objectivity, the first advantage of seniority.

Second, seniority is intuitively persuasive to many. Witness the behavior of the old hands when a new employee arrives. If they can, they will haze, break in, and orient the new person to *their* rights, *their* ways of doing things, and *their* status. They have the power to do this, at least informally. Moreover, they feel righteous about doing it. Unions did not invent seniority; they make use of its moral appeal. In a survey made in a large corporation of the basis for salaries paid managers, we came across a startling finding: among thirty plant managers whose performance had been objectively rated, pay levels had no correlation with ratings. Pay and total compensation were, however, well correlated with the number of years in the job. Managers, not unions, worked out that pay pattern.

A third argument for seniority is biological: 10 years in a job is an irreversible cost, 10 years out of someone's life. While the 20,000 hours perhaps were compensated, these are never just hours. They represent the exhaustion of an irreplaceable resource, time. Thus it could be argued (and is argued) that time is compensated on a flat hourly basis for a job (everyone receives the same pay per hour spent) and on a *longevity* basis for the loss of a person's life. If this is too subtle an argument, consider the decreasing options open to the aging, the increasingly vulnerable, and, in fact, the dying person (we do not mean to be morbid but to use "dying" in the sense that biologically one starts dying at 30) as time progresses.

Fourth, seniority means exposure to hazards such as accidents and stress: what one has endured. Is endurance the same as experience? It is regarded by many as a *form* of experience. "I am a part of all I have met" refers to the slings and arrows of fate, to travail, as well as to the benefits of experience in the form of increasing skills.

Fifth, up to a point seniority indeed brings an increase in skills in occupations in which time provides increasing opportunities to learn. True, not everyone learns from such opportunities, and 10 years may not be twice as good as 5. But the converse is convincing: no one can learn without opportunities.

Sixth, in some organizations survival in the job indicates at least minimum proficiency in the job and sometimes more than this.

Accrediting Experience?

If you were going to use these arguments to give a person credits, what would these credits be and how would different types of seniority be weighted? Consider the recent college policy of awarding such credits. Somewhat belatedly recognizing that adult students are an important constituency, many colleges are awarding credits for "life experience." These are actually credit hours toward a degree. Evidently the colleges feel able to set up tables of equivalence between courses and life experience. The above six arguments for seniority might be translated into giving credit for promotion or pay for:

1. Years spent in the occupation (Arguments 1, 3, and 5)

2. Years spent on the company payroll (Arguments 1, 2, 3, 4, and 6)

3. Decline in health, or biological aging in the occupation, measured as the difference between one's fitness and life expectancy on entering the job and one's present fitness and life expectancy (Arguments 3 and 4)

4. Actual exposure to physical hazards and emotional stress, if you can determine how to measure the latter by using alcoholism and other rates of stress for that occupation (Arguments 3 and 4)

5. Points awarded for opportunities to learn, if you can determine which jobs give the greatest number of opportunities, which training programs actually teach, and so on (Argument 5)

6. Points awarded for the number of years during which one might have been fired for nonperformance, if you can find a way to give greater credit for surviving under a quick-firing boss (Argument 6)

These points may not be exactly the union's or some managements' case for seniority. They are not a precise set of rules but rather a set of lines along which the Gray Panthers or other groups will likely adopt a fighting posture. Therefore, you should learn to think in these terms to defend youself. (Besides, we'll all be Gray Panthers eventually.)

A DEEPER VIEW OF EXPERIENCE

You will be responding to pressures on behalf of older managers, including some pressures along the above lines. At the same time, you can and should learn to think through assets along the most rational and productive lines possible. We can begin this search by looking at dictionary definitions of *experience*. There are at least a dozen. This ambiguity is one reason that behaviorists abandoned the broad idea of experience as a subjective phenomenon (for it they substituted more specific ideas such as rewards received for doing certain things—the laboratory animal's "experience" consists of a history of rewards received for performing certain actions). Among the dozen are six we find adaptable:

- Experience as practical work done
- Experience as "experting," that is, not only work done but work done well, as shown through a person's track record of results
- Experience as a set of skills acquired through working
- Experience as goals set or ventures undertaken
- Experience as what one has endured—stress or travail
- Experience as acquisition and declaration of values

Let us assume that you are going to devise a serious and practical system of credits for yourself or for others. This system, if comprehensive enough to touch all bases, should deal with each of the definitions above. To be fair, you *should* deal with each of them. For example, to credit a person only for work done while ignoring what has been done well is obviously biased to favor those who merely put in time.

RATIONAL EXPERIENCE

There are a number of components of rational experience.

The Résumé

The first component of rational experience is the objective job history. It is a summary of work. If an individual puts the history together, it is a "résumé." If he or she answers a set of standardized questions, it is an "application blank." At a minimum it includes a record of what the individual has done in the form of a series of statements such as "Jones was paid W to do Job X for Y years for Company Z."

What does each statement prove? In terms of the earlier discussion, such a statement is a seniority statement. Specifically, it is a seniority statement giving credit for an opportunity to learn or to hold a job, or both, for a given period of time, but not necessarily showing skill.

Anyone who offers such a self-description is making these seniority assumptions. No doubt a high earner will resent the suggestion that salary may not prove competence. It merely proves that the employee looked good enough to promote or hire and then proved not incompetent enough to demote or fire. Why is this so?

- Initial salary on a job is usually set according to two factors: what the *job* is considered to be worth and the employee's market value.

- In turn, market value depends on several factors other than performance. One of these is previous pay. When a new employer makes a job offer, it will rarely be less than the employee's previous level (if so, the employer probably will not make an offer at all) and normally not more than about 20 percent over that level.

- The employee's market value also depends on how many similar people there are who want the job. That factor often has nothing to do with the individual's ability.

The argument about the résumé or application blank is not that it should be ignored. Rather, greater care should be used in clarifying assumptions of what it measures about a person; the résumé mainly measures opportunity to learn—no small factor, but one we doubt is dominant among the six. But read on, and decide how you would weight the six.

Track Record

A manager is supposed to make things happen, to be an expert at obtaining *results* (indeed, the Latin word *experiri*, "to try," is the origin of the word *expert*). If the manager can point to particular objectives met, he or she can say what the track record is, which is far better than describing how the manager's time was spent, as on the résumé. George Odiorne and Edwin Miller (1966) wrote:

> There are two keys to pick the right man for a job: knowing the results the man has achieved on past jobs, and knowing the objectives of the job to be filled. If he has in the past achieved the results the present job is aiming for, he's the right man.

This principle, which may be so obvious that you may slide by it without thought, is behind talent decisions when you choose a quarterback or book a musician. Why not apply it to business? Many think they do, but when you look at the specific ways they go about identifying talent, it turns out that they are doing something else, such as judging talent from a résumé.

A track record is measured by the methods outlined in earlier chapters. As we indicated, it is measured in terms of only four fundamental operating results:

- Dollars, especially sales and finance
- Innovation
- Preservation of human and other assets
- Production

No doubt this list strikes some managers as too narrow. Where, for example, does data processing fit in? Does it not generate an operating result? The answer given before is still appropriate: data processing generates information, but this does not become an operating result unless it facilitates economic or innovative developments, the preservation of assets, or production decisions.

A broader definition of the track record was offered in terms of job elements in Chapter 7. The applicant or candidate offers evidence that he or she has done such work well. Some of this evidence will consist of reasons the person finds credible that he or she did achieve results. The interviewer also has to decide whether these reasons are credible.

From a review of the several hundred annual reports we have collected, we have found that managers and professionals offer the following reasons why they believe they have been effective in any given year. Some of these qualify as genuine results, as defined in this book, and some do not:

- "I opened a new branch office last year." This manager is describing a cost, not a result.

- "I kept within cost standards for the whole year." This is a result.

- "The branch office I opened was the first drive-in customer-servicing facility in the East." This is an innovative result.

- "I supervised 100 engineers." This is a workload, not a result.

- "I negotiated three major union contracts last year." This describes an opportunity to learn, not a result. Who knows but what the labor negotiator may have given the company away?

- "The new product I developed hit the market on time [not clearly a result] and did extremely well in sales its first year." This is closer to a result, though still vague.

Skills and Knowledge Acquired

A third definition of experience would be the lasting residual of the experiences described above. There are various ways to identify such effects of experience: relations with people, know-how, knowledge. As William James put it: "Experience molds us every hour and makes of our minds a mirror of the time-and-space connections between the things in the world."

The seasoned manager knows how to work the system, where things are located, who has the clout, and how to get to those people. The seasoned production superintendent knows that when the rate of the line slows down, it is often due to a neglected maintenance problem or to mistakes characteristic of a particular shift.

Some such knowledge can be appraised by asking the person, "How you would solve such and such a problem?" While this is a hypothetical question, the answer will often reveal whether the person understands the "space-and-time connections" which can produce a solution.

Résumé, Track Record, and Skills

The above three forms of experience are deliberately listed in this order. The first tells *what a person did;* the second, what he or she has to show for this work in *external results;* and the third, what he or she now has to show in *increments in know-how.*

Since we are most interested in the last form, what a person can do today, it might seem possible to forget the first two. We believe all three are necessary. History shows the experience which went into a person, while present skills can show only present evidence of the impact of that experience.

Rational Bias

However, if you think back to the arguments for seniority, you will find that the three forms account for only some of the arguments. Specifically, they do not account for biological aging or exposure to hazards. The emotional side of experience has been poorly described. We must go further in fully and properly accrediting experience.

EMOTIONAL ASPECTS OF EXPERIENCE

In contrast to the above aspects, the features now concerning us deal with *what we have experienced.* Rather than with experience as doing (according to the behaviorist view), we are now concerned with experience as it looks and feels from the inside (a humanistic view). Like the progression from résumé to skills, we see a progression from venturing to valuing as follows:

- Goals and commitments to action—ventures
- Persistence, endurance, and travail undergone in carrying out those commitments
- Lasting values formed in the experience

Goals and Ventures

Experientia, the Latin origin of the word *experience,* means "trial." People stick out their necks to see what will happen, venture and set goals, gamble or gambol. This analysis of a manager's history would inquire into past ventures, into what has been attempted. Such an inquiry is similar to the résumé, and yet there are crucial distinctions:

- Résumés tell merely what an individual did, normally carrying out the duties for which he or she was paid. They tone down the motivational side of work, the all-out characteristic, the zeal and energy expended.
- Venture histories tell what an individual attempted, the objectives set, not so much to show the intent of each duty as to show how high (or how sensible) the individual's sights were, how his or her effort was distributed (or concentrated) among different commitments.

Travail

Whereas experience is viewed above as an emotional gamble, here we consider the endurance of the manager who *hangs in there* during a long and difficult time. Until a manager does this, we don't really know his or her essential managerial qualities. This aspect of a manager's history describes the man or woman embattled, not the employee or the profitable entrepreneur. True, travail has something to do with results, but there are both similarities and distinctions:

- Results show what the manager has accomplished in tangible form.

- Travail shows what the manager has been willing to put out to get results; in this part of the history, experience is shown as much in failures and defeats as in successes.

Values

Finally, what is forged through experience is a set of strengths, things a manager is willing to fight for and considers of supreme importance. These are sometimes expressed as policies considered vital. Sometimes, values are shown only in combat—what a manager is willing to take a major risk for, put a job on the line for. Values are shown in the history but become progressively clear as the effects or end products of the experience, which finally forges a human being. They have something to do with skills and yet are very different:

- Skills are shown in and result from the manager's experience as its permanent end product, being expressed usually as *know-how.*

- Values are also shown in and are forged through experience, being expressed not as knowing in itself but as knowing *what is worth fighting for.*

The manager with superior values is superior to the manager with only know-how: the former may not waste time doing a certain thing at all, while the latter may devote considerable time to doing well something that need never have been attempted. Corporations need both types of manager, but corporate histories show us a greater number of disasters from bad valuing than from inefficiency.

Structure of Experience

If you want to characterize yourself or someone else in terms of a well-rounded portrait of experience, answer questions in the order shown in numbered boxes in Table 8–1. If you cannot give convincing evidence in each box, the history is deficient.

USING ACCOUNTS OF EXPERIENCE

There are several practical uses of these ideas of experience. One of them—learning how to use your own experience more fully—will be discussed in Chapter 9. Here we will confine ourselves to the uses of others' experience.

In general, accounts of experience should be the major tool for appraising a person. The following situations are among those in which we may want to do that:

- The treatment of hiring and promoting at high levels (Chapters 6 and 7) discussed the use of a person's résumé and track record (Boxes 1 and 2 in Table 8–1), broadened in this chapter to comprise four additional features of a person's experience.

- Assessment centers: we will discuss below how these are improved by the use of accounts of experience.

- Equal opportunity: the accreditation of experience is a special problem and a special opportunity for avoiding or minimizing bias.

- Management trainees: younger candidates have special problems, which are discussed below.

- Overspecialization: many of a person's most important skills and values are ignored by bureaucratic ground rules, as shown below.

TABLE
8–1

THE STRUCTURE OF EXPERIENCE

Experience as opportunity   *Experience as realization*

Rational experience	1. Résumé What has been done, where, at what pay, and for how long?	2. Results What do you have to show for this work which was of benefit to others?	3. Know-how What can you now demonstrate in the form of skills, know-how, and knowledge?
Emotional experience	4. Ventures What have you tried to do—what risks, gambles, or gambols?	5. Stress What have you endured in pressure, in travail—what can you take? What disasters?	6. Values What have you shown you are willing to fight for and persist toward?

Assessment Centers

By an assessment center we mean a center for the appraisal of managers by giving them simulated tasks to do under observation. Trained observers, usually other managers, evaluate their performance against agreed-on criteria. A typical assessment-center task for individuals would give a manager an inbox full of mail and ask him or her to sort the contents by priority for response and to indicate what his or her response is. The priority judgments and responses are evaluated by the assessor. Another typical task consists of a group exercise in which six managers are given blocks to assemble, under time pressure, to match a certain structure. The observers note how well the managers size up the task, who leads and communicates and who follows effectively, and whether as a team they succeed. In previous chapters we mentioned the values of assessment centers. Our concern here is with weaknesses in the centers which may be remedied by the use of accounts of experience. Primarily, these accounts are useful for the following:

- *Evaluating a manager's actual skills.* The account of experience provides evidence that the manager has in fact applied the skills on the job which are shown in the assessment center. This would appear to be an important demonstration. However, the center provides the chance to demonstrate skills for which the person may never have had on-the-job opportunity.

- *Validating the center's conclusions.* By carefully gathered, verified, and evaluated accounts of experience, assessment-center conclusions can be tested. Promotion rates have been offered to show that assessment centers are valid; that is, persons rated highly get promoted faster. For reasons given in Chapter 6, this is not a sufficient criterion.

- *Providing simple justice.* To the extent that a manager is given a chance to prepare an account of experience, he or she is treated more justly than if observed only during 3 days at a center. Remember that the manager will consider that many years on the job provides a better test than 3 days in a center.

Equal Opportunity

The use of a résumé sharply restricts the population to be considered for a job. Thus, some companies have recognized that they should no longer set lengthy requirements (such as 10 years' experience) for a job. The résumé (Box 1, Table 8–1) should be deemphasized. However, this change in no way needs to lessen the chances of a minority-group member or a woman for a job. The other areas of experience can be emphasized in equal-opportunity cases:

CASE
8-2

EXPERIENCE COMES IN MANY PACKAGES

A woman wanting to go back to work after her husband's early retirement due to an illness was considered for the job of production scheduler. She had "no production experience" in her résumé. What she had was 12 years as a housewife. A somewhat thorough personnel interviewer decided to find out what is covered in the broad role of housewife. Through an account of experience, the interviewer learned about the applicant's 12 years of raising six children, nursing three aging parents, and tending an army of cats. He especially learned why she was famous in her husband's company for giving the periodic banquet. She planned the menu for twenty people, supervised the buying, and directly baked, broiled, fried, and assembled foods on an extraordinarily intricate production schedule so that all hot foods emerged at once. The interviewer concluded that she had had production experience.

- *Results.* Instead of asking the black candidate to present years of experience of which he or she is likely to be short, you can ask what the candidate has to show for the kind and duration of experience that he or she *can* present. The same can be applied to women: stop asking candidates to prove over and over that they lack conventional experience but allow them to present the experience that they *do* have. See Case 8-2.

- *Ventures.* Instead of asking a black candidate to present only jobs held (for which the record may be spotty or limited), find out what he or she has tried to do. The courage of a venture may be a more important qualification for blacks and women than the formal credentials they may lack.

- *Persistence and travail.* In our society, the disadvantaged have had to weather the storms of discouragement. Who is to say that tenacity, if it can be shown by a disadvantaged candidate, is less important than formal credentials or skills? Older employees, too, can often present evidence of persistence missing in the young.

- *Values.* At this point in history, many women and minority-group members are showing a new assertiveness. The question should not be whether they are "too aggressive" (as it is often put) but what it is they are aggressive *about*. Aggressiveness and assertiveness represent human energy, and the question is whether it has been directed into channels which can be productive. This question is answerable only through a study of the person's history.

Management Trainees

The authors had the opportunity to discuss with a large number of Dartmouth students their status as potential management trainees. It turned out that many were not considering business careers, not only because they were critical of business values but chiefly because they felt that they had had "no experience." It is simply untrue that a 19-year-old college student has had no experience. What is true is that the student's experience has not been evaluated, except in a formal, credentialed way (Case 8–3).

Overspecialization

The same unreal limitation of opportunity is very often imposed on managers and résumés. Once a person gets slotted as an overseas manager, he or she is often considered no longer a stateside manager. Or an engineer in high-altitude instrumentation is not understood to be able to learn some other kind of instrumentation, once the first line of work is played out.

You can avoid these wastes of talent, in which an able person is prevented from entering another line of work laterally or moving up vertically because of certain specializations considered to slot him. There are two ways to avoid talent waste:

- Insist on evidence from all six kinds of experience and not merely from the first kind.

- Start elsewhere than in Box 1.

HOW CAN SOMEBODY HAVE "NO EXPERIENCE"?

A Dartmouth student was reluctant to apply for a position as production clerk to learn the soft-drink business from the ground up because he had had "no experience." The dean was struck by the contrast between this notion of no experience and the student's activities in the previous summer. The high point of his years at Dartmouth was his leadership of a complicated mountain-climbing expedition. The group was to get to the top of a difficult and dangerous peak. The student supervised the purchase of $12,000 worth of equipment for the group of ten, trained the group in safety procedures, evaluated the physical fitness of each, rejecting two, and led the group on the successful expedition.

Let us consider what this second recommendation amounts to. The usual net cast for qualified candidates considers only people with 5 years of a certain kind of experience plus, say, a college education. Only those who can present these credentials are permitted to show what results, skills, ventures, persistences, and values they can present as evidence of total qualification.

Instead of this undue emphasis on the résumé, we open up candidacy along alternative routes. The new advertisement reads, not "5 years plus a degree," but something like this:

> We are looking for a plant manager, textiles. If you worked for such a plant, in a fairly responsible position for 3 years or more, you might consider the criteria below. However, if you worked in some *other* position you think might be equivalent or which put the same general kind of responsibilities on you, you might want to consider this job also. Either way, be prepared to prove how your past experience:
>
> - Involved you in constructive labor relations, cost control, and quality control using out-of-date equipment.

- Proved you can take on difficult challenges, stay with an operation under discouraging conditions, and deliver top results.

A POPULATION FORECAST

Demographers have forecast that during the next few decades the proportion of aging people will greatly increase. This is exactly the connotation we think is biased and misleading. It divides the population into "people" and "aging people." We are all aging. But that absurdity is not the main problem.

We prefer to speak of the proportion of "seasoned" people increasing. We insist that experience has values which not only have been unmeasured and ignored but have been screened out by the employment funnel's narrowness regarding the definition of experience.

Six applicable definitions have been offered. Three have to do with a person's functioning and how it may be enhanced through exposure to experience. Three others have to do with a person's experiencing and what our reconstruction shows that the person can try for, endure, and fight for.

ESCAPE FROM TRIVIALITY

It is our suspicion that the more specific, measurable, and objective our data are about a person, especially the certification given by a college, the records of employment in the personnel office, and most test scores, the more trivial they often are. What this means is that to evaluate properly the most vital aspects of experience—ventures, tenacity, and values—takes more trouble than to evaluate reliably the least vital. Most large organizations are unlikely to go to this amount of trouble. What that means follows.

Experience will make a comeback, and this is good. But unless our recommended option—that we learn to identify and honor the assets of seasoned people—is followed, society will merely assert the rights of senior employees because they are *older,* not because they are seasoned. We leave it to you to estimate the impact on productivity and self-respect.

ACTION SUGGESTIONS

Here are a few suggestions for action:

- Feature the accomplishments of senior people, not their seniority. This can be done through publicity and recognition. Fewer gold watches for longevity, please.

- Take a look at the bonus system. Is it oriented primarily to contributions which only younger people can make?

- Break up age ghettos. Look at your organization charts. Develop policies and procedures to assure an interesting age mix so that seasoned people can contribute to the learning of junior people, and vice versa.

- Don't let insurance premiums determine how your organization makes use of, hires, or promotes senior people. Insurance does not have the aim of telling you who you can hire and promote, but companies have been allowing this to happen.

9

MAKE YOUR OWN EXPERIENCE COUNT

Experience will make a comeback—that is to the good. But favors for seniority will be due to pressure groups—that sounds like a mixed blessing. Unfortunately this is the way in which things work in large bureaucracies. So let us turn, more hopefully, to the least bureaucratic unit in your organization: you, as an individual, or more specifically your own career.

No doubt you have learned a great deal from experience and may even agree with the opinion here that it is your leading asset. But the truth is that if you work the way Henry Mintzberg (1973) found that managers work, you have not taken the time to sift through your experience and learn what its assets are. This would be especially true if all you can do is write a résumé. As Table 8–1, "The Structure of Experience," showed, that is only the beginning of what experience means and is the least important indicator of assets.

TIME BIAS

Your career is made up of three times, past, present, and future. Some of us are preoccupied with one of these times to the neglect of the other two. We pay a price for this neglect. The *crisis manager* is always buried in the present, without time to plan or to take a good

TAKE TIME TO LEARN WHY THERE'S ALWAYS A CRISIS

In 1965 I was working on the development of a new product both as project engineer and as a contributor to the circuit design. I allowed the program to fall behind schedule by failing to admit my inability to handle both jobs successfully and by simply working longer and longer hours "putting out fires" without backing off to look at the whole problem and ask for help. I felt that I had worked extraordinarily hard and was shocked to receive an unenthusiastic review because of my lack of judgment. This was a valuable lesson.

look to evaluate products, programs, or people (Case 9–1). The *anxious manager*, preoccupied with the future, is never able to enjoy today's success but wonders how long it can continue. He or she is a chronic doubter who believes management's outlook should be dour, if not sour. The *rigid manager* cannot forget yesterday's failures or successes. The hearing aid is turned off for today, and there is no imagination about the future. He or she is a know-it-all whom subordinates cannot reach with a bright idea. The door is closed

Some managers ask whether reviewing their experience will not make them rigid. On the contrary, inflexible managers have only a narrow idea of their experience. George Santayana said, "Those who cannot remember the past are condemned to repeat it." Do not confuse the review of experience with preoccupation with the past. What actually happens when we take managers through a consciousness-raising exercise regarding the past is that they learn that the past is not a closed book. For example, they see new possibilities in the present and future.

The reason for this self-renewal is that, through reminiscence about the past, managers rediscover old values and talents that recently have not been felt or used. In short, they find that they have many more resources of energy and know-how than they are

REFLECT ON SUCCESS SO YOU CAN MAKE IT HAPPEN AGAIN

In January 1972, the chairman of the board said that we should have a program to ensure that all personnel would have their salary reviews on time. If there was any slippage in a review, the system or program would notify the wage and salary department so that it could initiate action to get the review accomplished. The project was assigned to me and at first glance seemed rather straightforward. However, upon examination, much had to be changed by EDP, wage and salary, industrial relations, offset printing, payroll, and all managers who processed salary reviews and changes in the plant.

Because of the complexity of the changes involved and the large number of personnel who had to be notified within a rather short time, I chose to document the new program and make presentations to various groupings of management personnel. I gave eighteen presentations to a total of 335 management and supervisory personnel within a week and a half.

I must have some theatrical blood in me—I thoroughly enjoyed the presentations. I think part of the source of the good feelings I had in the presentations was a function of the thorough way in which the program was laid out and the way in which the presentations were made. There were very few questions from the floor that we hadn't anticipated, and even those were easy to answer because of my knowledge of the subject.

The program was instituted without problems and is still going strong today. . . .

now tapping. The reason is that the present job is usually defined so narrowly that few managers do not feel constrained by the organizational setting. It may be necessary so to limit action, but jobs need not limit self-perception. To put it another way, managers who have gone through experience inventories feel self-renewal (Case 9–2).

How does a manager take an inventory of experience so that more possibilities in the present and future open up? This is the question to which this chapter will outline answers. Suggestions will be made in the light of observation of several hundred managers and engineers who have gone through what we call "experience enhancement." The basic idea is that experience can pay double: at the time you have it, you learn something; later, on reflection, you learn still more.

HOW PEOPLE LEARN OR FAIL TO LEARN FROM EXPERIENCE

Experience may be the best teacher, but if so, it seems to be an unreliable teacher. Otherwise, all managers with 10 years' seniority would have equal knowledge, provided they had the same opportunities to learn. But even among learners in one classroom (or any other learning environment, including football fields, tennis courts, and even the dance floor) individual differences are impressive.

Stop for a moment and consider how people learn as well as how well they learn. They evidently do not all learn in the same way. Some learn from abstract theory, including what they read and study. Others learn from deliberate experiments, by trying out something and observing the outcome. Still others simply throw themselves into action and learn without a design. And others learn by reflecting afterward on whatever happened.

In a complex business operation, all four styles are necessary for learning. When you set a program objective, it is a hypothetical blueprint for the future, a theory which must yet be proved. After launching the program, you eventually will receive data on the practical effects of the theory. But along with these criteria (fairly precise facts which test the theory) you will obtain broader observations about your theory's practical effects and the conditions under which they come about. Finally, at a later date, when all the facts and related observations have come in, you can reflect on the whole operation and put the pieces together.

The delays between these steps in an operation may be lengthy or short, but for the purposes of this chapter the important delay is between Steps 1 and 4:

1. State the objective and launch the program.

2. Gather precise data on the criteria that show how well the program is working.

3. While giving the program a chance to work, allow yourself to get other serendipitous observations in addition to the original criteria, including casual reports from people in the field.

4. After all the results are in and enough time has lapsed for the dust to settle and your own perspective to grow, look at the program as a whole. What caused things to happen, and what did you learn?

The delay between initial action and final result, between Steps 1 and 4, is what makes annual reports or reports at even longer intervals necessary. It makes working accounts not only desirable for improving communications but essential so that the entire program can be laid out and cause be matched to effect.

Learning Bias

Some managers boast of being practical. Sometimes this means that they pay attention only to Step 2. Others are intuitive and rely on impressions; they pay attention only to Step 3 and look down on other managers, whom they believe lacking in "creativity." Still others are so tightly focused on management by objectives (Step 1) that they neglect hard-nosed evaluation (Step 2) and serendipitous or casual learning (Step 3). Obviously, we believe that you can profitably use all these styles and should do so.

Effective Learning

The laboratory concept of learning stresses Steps 1 and 2. Those who believe people learn best through field trials will insist on the importance of both Steps 2 and 3. In this chapter the focus is on Step 4. This learning from the experience as a whole, at a sufficient interval after having had it, is likely to show you different things

AN ATTORNEY DECIDING WHERE HIS REAL ASSETS ARE

After a tour with the Army as an attorney, I returned to the law firm that I had been associated with prior to entering the Army. Shortly after my return, two members, partners when I had left, left the firm to form a new partnership (a partnership had been promised me when I first went with the firm, but it had not yet materialized). This event led, within 3 months, to discussions on forming a partnership of the remaining four members and the two associates (myself and one other). In open discussions evaluations were made of the pluses and minuses of the potential members and associates. My evaluation indicated some of the following: my trial experience, though limited to 18 months in private practice (the military experience of more than 300 trials was excluded), was thought to be outstanding, especially in logical presentation, jury presence, and ability to think well under pressure and on my feet; I was complimented on being a comer. My ability to bring in clients was thought to be high, and I related to people well. It was thought that my enthusiasm had declined since my first year with the firm and that I wasn't working as hard as I could but that I was doing a "good" job. In explanation, it's important to note that the Army had severely dampened my desire to continue to be a trial attorney and had opened a new potential career as a business attorney. The loss of two good men (who were good friends and sharp attorneys) dampened my enthusiasm and desire for a partnership. After much soul-searching and discussion I decided to turn down the partnership offer and seek employment as a business attorney. This occurred within 10 months after I had returned to private practice.

from what you see during the action, especially during Steps 2 and 3. Without denying that all four steps have something to teach, we are concerned in this chapter with what your whole career can teach you about what you are good at doing and what you think is worth doing. This process is called experience enhancement. It is a way to turn your seniority into experience and your experience into assets. The premises are:

1. Experience is an asset and contains resources.

MAKING A FAILURE VALUABLE BY LEARNING FROM IT

Four years ago, as a "new hire" for the company, I found myself overeager during one of my first calls. I had been given a map, a car, a territory, and some sales objectives, as well as order forms, and told, "Go get 'em." I walked into a small firm, and the manager ignored me as if I didn't exist. I kept trying to get his attention and finally lost my patience and told him I'd leave the materials. He picked them up and dropped them in his waste can. From that point on things got worse. The wrong step cost me the account's support on all my programs.

2. It may be inventoried, invested, and used more fully (Case 9–3).

3. The very act of taking this inventory can expand these resources (Case 9–4).

THE ADVANTAGES OF EXPERIENCE

The intent is to help managers get more from their experience. It is not only the original experience, or opportunity to learn, but also the second wave of profit taking from it which develops individuals of superior merit. Many of the advantages you have in life fade with age. An engineering degree becomes obsolete in 9 years, as an MIT president once said. Your fitness declines as your belt size grows. Employability drops for most of us beyond 35. The one asset which age can increase, that of experience, is not allowed to expand if given too narrow a definition.

Expanding your concept of what experience is and bringing it to life so that you can put your finger on it will occur if:

• You know what has happened (Case 9–5).

GETTING SMARTER REQUIRES REVIEWING WHAT HAPPENED

I do not have much political sense and often play into the hands of people who are equally ambitious. I am the manager of quality control. I am at the same level as the manager of operations. He and I are both aggressive and talented and are pushing to the top. Operations needed a production control manager. I felt that I could do a great job and that the post would help my résumé, even though it was one level below my present job. I asked my rival for the job, working for him, and explained how my present job could be reorganized to require less responsibility and be handled by one of my subordinates. His answer was that he would not consider me for the production control job, but that inasmuch as I was willing to work for him as PC manager, why wouldn't I just shift quality control under him and work for him there?

I hope I'll get smarter.

- You examine your experience at sufficient intervals to make a full evaluation—to see the event as a whole (Case 9-6).

- You reconstruct the event or events in enough detail to permit you to conjecture some valid reasons for what happened and what it means today.

These steps are customarily neglected in the order named. Most of us can say roughly what has happened, especially recently. Memory begins to deprive us of what happened yesterday; we are interested only in the current. We resist the idea of learning from what is past; after all, it is "water over the dam"—let's cut our losses and go on from here. Such policies, if pushed too far, deprive managers of the chance to develop their major assets.

SAMPLE APPROACHES TO THE ENHANCEMENT OF EXPERIENCE

Can managers learn to learn from experience? Yes, if they are convinced that experience has a potential value to them and if they

OFTEN A FULL EVALUATION CAN COME ONLY LATER

I may expect too much of others. The ultimate utilization of a successfully completed research project depends to a large extent on our ability to gain acceptance by operating divisions. For example, we completed the research phase of an office copier and depended on marketing people and product planners to provide us with inputs to ensure that product features were appropriate and that the required investment was acceptable. That information came very late in the program and contributed to its cancellation. Since we had spent about $200,000 on the project, cancellation came as a major blow. I felt somewhat bitter at the time, but now I see it as a valuable experience. Now, to the extent that I am able, I make it my own responsibility to see that all relevant information, marketing and economic as well as technical, is available when needed and is evaluated.

---

are given a proper method. By now you have made up your mind whether you are going to find out what value lies in your unexamined past experience. May we suggest a useful method? Here are some methods we have tried in the past:

Critical Incidents

In a laboratory setting, pairs of managers practice reporting recent incidents of success and failure to one another. The critique given immediately afterward by the listener asks whether the reporter has given enough details to provide a well-rounded picture of why and how the incident occurred, under what circumstances, and so on (Cases 9–7 and 9–8).

Annual Reports

In a similar laboratory setting, managers practice reconstructing last year's results. Such an exercise begins by telling a partner the

LOOK AT INCIDENTS TO DIAGNOSE YOUR STYLE

The following incidents led to an interesting discussion about management style. One manager said: "Just the other day I was going to the store, and I thought I should take my cleaning and drop it off, pay my utilities, get gas, take merchandise back to another store, etc. It got to the point that I was doing so many things that I forgot to go the store I originally planned to visit. Just yesterday, while critiquing a standard cost procedure, I kept getting off on little points which were external to the procedure, but I kept bringing them up, hoping to solve them at the same time.

"Made a sandwich yesterday, was frying the egg, toasting the toast, frying the bacon, talking on the phone, and trying to eat a cookie all at the same time.

"Do I do too many things at once?"

objectives set at the start of the year and then includes the objectives which were added during the year. The manager attempts to explain the good and poor results (Case 9–9). The feedback gives a critique of how complete and convincing the reporter's account is.

Track Record Interview

Managers conduct a track record interview following the outline given in Chapter 7. If the exercise is run during a management training workshop, they can simulate "applying" to a peer for their present jobs. The peer then judges each "applicant" by the adequacy and convincing details presented to show why the applicant considers himself or herself qualified for certain areas of the present job.

Journals

The manager keeps a journal, recording at least one positive incident and one negative incident, the high and low points of each

CASE
9–8

VENTILATING IRRITATION

The following incident provoked a discussion with this engineer's boss: "When I first came to this company, there was a policy to drive around the maintenance building to the parking area. There was a driveway leading to the parking lot that was an exit. It was always wide open (you could see clearly both directions), and cars usually were not coming out in the morning. I would drive the wrong way up the driveway to the parking lot because it was faster and just as safe. Some employees reported me for doing something against the policy. Some of the policies and procedures that an organization has purely stink, and I am fed up with them, but rather than spend my time changing them, sometimes I go ahead and just disobey them."

---

week. Periodically the manager reviews the journal to see what recurring competences and limitations are shown (Case 9–10).

Biography

The manager writes a series of annual reports covering the last decade and asks a peer to help him or her spot any trends found in several of these reports. A trend would consist of a competence which is increasing or decreasing or a value which is felt more and more strongly or less and less so.

How do such exercises enrich learning? Depending on the time span reviewed, the exercises emphasize reflective learning from experience. Thus they appear to make a person more intuitive (hence less practical) and more introverted (hence less oriented to the outside world). They also appear to strengthen the holistic (systems) view of performance because they are historical rather than analytical.

These surmises are true in the sense that extroverted managers have more difficulty with the approaches than do introverts, and practical people resist them more than do intuitive people. How-

LEARNING FROM FAILURE STARTS WITH ADMITTING IT

In 1970 I was reassigned to another store. I was opposed to the move for several reasons, but it was part of a total district plan, and my district manager requested me to take over this store. For the first time since I had worked for this company I did not feel totally committed. My disappointment was reflected in my facial expression, and it was obvious to the associates I did not belong as part of the new store. Since the store had previously been managed in a different style than mine, my problems became compounded. My attitude was reflected in the total commitment, and I never did achieve the results for the company that my ability and experience, plus that of the associates in the store, predicted. I think I can say I learned more about myself in those 6 months than in any other assignment. I finally faced up to the fact that I had failed in that assignment.

ever, there is a way to run such exercises that enriches the experience of anyone.

Match managers in pairs who are likely to learn different things from an experience. The thoughtful introvert will teach the spontaneous extrovert, and vice versa. For example, a critical incident reconstructed by an introvert will ordinarily tell more about how he or she went about succeeding or failing than about the motives of others or the role of the environment. A critique of the incident should point this out, and the introvert can begin to enrich his or her experience by including more of the motives of others in it.

Or match an idea person with a realist. If a manager reconstructs an annual report which is long on creativity and innovation and short on hard-nosed practical consequences and causes, the hard-nosed partner's critique of the report should show how it could be enriched with commonsense details. In running the exercises listed, match opposites; they will clash but will teach each other more.

KEEPING A JOURNAL KEEPS SOME MANAGERS GOING

A manager wrote in his journal, summing up as follows: "When I was promoted to assistant district manager, I was transferred to the Long Island area, 1 hour and 45 minutes from my home. I was forced to stay overnight several times a week, which caused family pressures. I was put into an area that doesn't particularly take to "outsiders." I was also under the pressure of learning two new departments during this period. I was constantly being challenged for my ability. I approached my district manager for guidance—he was going to help me in my training because of his background, but he had problems of his own. Besides being a low point of my career, I also consider this an experience that I would repeat tomorrow if I had to. I feel I am learning more about operations and training and people than in all my years before."

MANAGERS' RESPONSE TO EXPERIENCE ENHANCEMENT

We have run such exercises many times, with several hundred managers and engineers in a dozen organizations. How did they respond? What they liked best and found most revealing included these features of experience enhancement:

- The methods, especially the critical incidents, could be used back on the job.

- The process of experience enhancement put the ball back into the individual manager's court, where manager development belongs, according to many managers.

- From the reconstruction of past experience, the individual saw assets of his or hers which had been forgotten and had not been used lately.

Not all managers and engineers liked and enjoyed the process. Among the objections to some of the procedures were:

- Stopping to look at something that is going well is sometimes disconcerting, and reviewing a distant past failure is often seen as crying over spilt milk.

- The procedures involve too much writing; many managers and engineers dislike and actively avoid writing.

This criticism can be avoided by choosing carefully the time at which experience enhancement is attempted. If a manager is very busy and holds many winning hands (a "fast track" manager, for example), this is not the right time to stop and question his or her momentum. On the other hand, such a momentum continued indefinitely may create a workaholic. "Success" is not a good excuse for never examining one's life.

A manager who has had many serious defeats will inevitably conduct such a self-examination as we recommend. The question, then, is whether to conduct it comprehensively and creatively. The problem of timing, again, is paramount. An acutely depressed manager is in no condition to conduct a comprehensive, creative examination of his or her career. The recommendation is that every manager learn how to review experience but apply the methods when somewhat (if not totally) "up." When very much "down," he or she should wait if possible.

This points to the greater problem. The pure conversationalist among managers, who neglects any records other than pure accounting or other facts, is at the mercy of memory and is not analytical enough to make much sense out of what is happening. Some managers of this type like to "meet" all day and confirm one another's prejudices and assumptions. They will resist keeping even a brief journal, at least initially, but at a later point they may find that the rich details have fascination and value.

Perhaps it is possible to learn to keep written accounts by dictating them. A problem in dictating is the thoughtless rattling off of an account which really deserves more critical analysis and reflection.

In the sample approaches to experience enhancement, one

method involved managers giving one another accounts. In this way, they taught each other to write as well as to review experience. In the end, it is the latter goal which is important, although we frankly doubt that it can be attained without facing up to the necessity of becoming a top historian of one's own experiences.

ACTION SUGGESTIONS

Here are a couple of suggestions for action:

- Instead of annual reviews, try a session in which there are no bosses. Just pair off managers who do not work for one another. Have them "review" each other's performance.

- If that works, try a more ambitious version of the same thing, covering the last 5 years.

10

WHAT NEEDS TO BE DONE?

We have explored several situations requiring good judgment as if they were unrelated. Stepping back now, we can more readily see the system as a coherent whole. The coherence among the fifteen specific projects described in this chapter should provide momentum toward these goals:

- Extending the influence of line management
- Using the micromap to increase good judgment
- Hiring for results, hence improving the quality of the work force
- Promoting for results, hence turning the organization around or pushing it forward
- Increasing the value given experience

These fifteen are projects that you can handle yourself, delegate if you back them, or advocate if you are a staff executive. An early question that might be raised about the line orientation is, "Should chief executives acquire greater influence?" Organization theorists raise doubts about the centralization of power. Those doubts will be aggravated by our goal of extending the influence of line managers.

Throughout the book, however, there are concepts which have made clear the power of a performer to make or break a superior by giving or depriving that superior of knowledge of the operation. Our proposal is to increase the power of every performer by turning as many people as possible into managers. We further propose to increase their power as managers by requiring their immediate superiors to *negotiate* with them. Finally, we propose to increase performers' power by enabling them to advocate their own sense of worth and to initiate working accounts. We conceive of a job as a domain in which the worker is the supreme authority as to what really happens and why.

While line influence over the operation should be increased, the power of performers is also to be increased. How can this be? The influence of every line manager over results, not people, should be increased. Autocracy is not advocated. Autocracy arises out of the boss's inability to know what is going on; the boss attempts to hide this ignorance, first from others and then, in extreme cases, from himself or herself. The final result of that dismal sequence is an attempt to rule by uninformed directives. This kind of power is reduced by the system described here.

EXTEND THE INFLUENCE OF LINE MANAGERS

We urge you to replace the traditional performance review with a new system built around working accounts. You say, "But we have already installed MBO." This means that you have started moving in the direction of PA-2. MBO requires accountability for results, as we do, but it needs to go further.

Let's review the rationale for the working account. In management jobs, there is often a gap between decision and results. This gap forces a longer-range accountability than many acknowledge. This long range, in turn, forces the use of historical reconstruction and documentation. The documentation must be more than quick-rating forms and checklists of objectives. It is not provided by the traditional operating report, which is not rich enough to show causation.

Even in the very short run, when an action produces immediate results, we prefer the critical incident to the pure operating report and performance rating. In the longer run, the annual report and the track record are distinctly preferable to the traditional alternatives. A track record is better for promotion, for example, than a set of psychological test scores.

Even if this rationale is convincing, line managers will use a new system only if it produces a payoff visible to them. That payoff lies in the extension of their influence. PA-1 certainly did not provide much influence over operating results, but will PA-2 do so?

The steps recommended are designed to assure that a new system will extend that influence and to show the general manager at the top that it does so. It will do so if only because the general manager (or president or other chief executive of the unit in which the PA-2 system is to be adapted) will adapt the system to his or her operating needs. Only if the system is so perceived by line managers will it be accepted down the line from the chief executive who first installs it.

If you are a personnel executive, this plan will sound as if you should get out of the performance-appraisal business and turn it over to the line. There is some truth in this assumption. Many personnel executives are concerned that line managers fight their PA system and know that the line must buy into such a system in order to use it. But the executives are unwilling to let go of this territory long enough for someone else to occupy it. Actually, accountability for riding herd on a system change of this magnitude, as well as on the related systems that are recommended, properly belongs to personnel executives.

Here are some specific projects to help you design, pilot-test, and provide a way to move your organization away from PA-1 and toward a line-oriented system of PA:

1. *With immediate subordinates, the highest-ranking line execu-*

tive develops a system of working accounts and extends that system downward. For example, just as the chief executive is accountable to the board, he or she requires annual and related reports from each immediate subordinate. The reports form the major segments of the chief executive's own annual report. These working accounts resemble, but are to be distinguished from, the operating reports that no doubt were required in the past. (If this distinction is not clear, reconsider the discussion in Chapter 2.) If an MBO system is already in effect, broaden and deepen the report and the discussion until it qualifies as a working-account system.

After the system of working accounts at the top satisfies the chief executive, extend it downward in the same manner. Among the criteria for satisfaction would be the following:

- An open discussion has been facilitated.

- Feelings as well as facts have been clarified.

- The causes of the results have become clearer.

- The individual contributions of subordinates have become easier to assess.

- The extent to which both parties hinder or help each other has been freely described and clarified.

Continue to extend the system downward as long as line managers believe that it repays the effort more than does the PA-1 system now in effect. Where the greater payoff of the new system is agreed upon, PA-1 is discontinued. For example, throw away your rating forms. However, retain your annual reports and other working accounts and the evaluations of them. These ratings, which tell how qualified evaluators look at an individual's results and the relevance of his or her activities to those results, replace the old ratings of good conduct, traits, or intuitive impressions.

2. *Train everyone to work for someone.* Working for someone is supposed to be a skill people acquire on their first jobs. Perhaps this is why many strongly believe that the secret of a meteoric

career is working early for a good boss. However, bosses who teach people how to work for someone are in a minority.

An outline of such a program was given in Chapter 2. It is related to Project 11 below: training people to write and speak on behalf of their own work. But Project 2 consists in clarifying and practicing two related skills: (*a*) helping make someone over you a success and (*b*) influencing that person in your own interest. Many may think they know how to influence others, but managers have often told us that they feel helpless when faced with an "impossible" boss. Such statements testify to the importance of this project.

3. *Train everyone in negotiating working accounts with a subordinate.* There are hundreds of training programs in how to supervise, and we do not propose to add to their number. In fact, those programs are concerned not with the conduct of an "organic inquiry" (see Project 5 below) but only with well-known bread-and-butter skills in supervision. That is not what this book is about.

Project 3 concerns something very different and more specific: how to obtain, analyze, verify, and clarify through discussion the meaning of working accounts. Specifically, this means critical incidents, annual reports, and track records. Also included would be the simple and practical procedure of developing a better consensus of what is expected on a particular job (see Chapter 5).

USING THE MICROMAP

The blueprint for the short-run account of performance is the micromap (Figure 10–1). At least two people, the performer and the observer, follow the map. One of the main points of the map is that the two necessarily see different aspects of it. Thus they must work together and combine their separate realities to produce a complete map. In spite of this necessary collaboration, the micromap as a tool is more helpful to the observer, who is responsible for aiding the performer to get the work out in coordination with others.

The first thing to do is to replace other, very faulty maps with

Figure
10-1

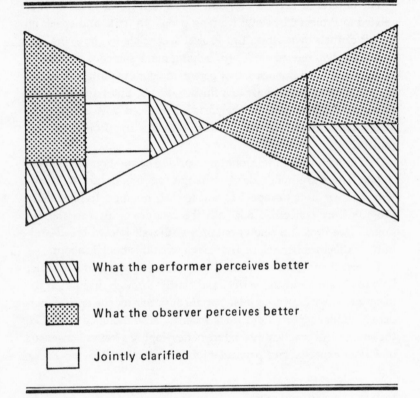

	What the performer perceives better
	What the observer perceives better
	Jointly clarified

the micromap. One such map is the job description, which is faulty if it lists only duties. Duties, which are the content of Area 7, can show only a fraction of the reality of performance. Also to be replaced are performance ratings, which engage supervisors in a fallacious numbers game, requiring them to rate things they cannot observe and obligating them to fake ratings and thus lose respect for the form itself.

Second, using a better map requires deciding what you are paying for. This is what should be quantified. If you are paying for the performance of duties, PA-1 will probably suffice, but if you are paying for the accomplishment of results, you need PA-2. Once these results have been clarified, they should be evaluated by a person who is in a position to do so. Since our concept of a result is a visible effect on others, other people must evaluate an individual's performance outcomes. The person on the organization chart as the performer's boss is not always the proper evaluator of outcomes. Neither is the boss of the boss.

Use of the micromap, then, requires that we rate (V) only what we pay for and the likelihood (P) with which the performer's actions produced that result. The brief "formula" is "Quantify only (V×P) for results within the judging zone."

Many processes of importance to managers, especially feedback loops, can be discerned on the micromap. Some are completed by the observer, and some by the performer. Sometimes mysteries of low motivation and poor morale are cleared up when we see what the loops are showing the performer. The micromap thus depicts a *multiple-loop* situation, in contrast to the single loop supposed by traditional performance review and by the narrower forms of learning theory.

These remarks about feedback loops and other ways of analyzing performance are oriented to a new form of quantification which we have outlined only in principle and certainly not specifically. Getting rid of inappropriate numbers, however, is useless unless performer and observer use words to represent what is important to them. What we called an organic inquiry into the causes of performance is as much concerned with the use of words as it is with the use of numbers. This is the main virtue of the working account: it is a blend of words and numbers. How does the working account make the organic inquiry with words possible?

A working account is enriched by including both feelings and specific details. Because the enriched account can detect the causes of results which might otherwise escape us, it makes causal analysis possible. At the same time, it is inevitably more wordy and strains the patience of a manager who would rather make a rating even if it means nothing than think through an extended report which contains a meaning to be discovered by hard thinking.

Specific projects for developing managers' causal analysis include the following:

4. *Decide for each job what you are paying for. If you are paying for results, use the micromap system. If not, leave the job under the PA-1 system.* If jobs do not generate results or if no one knows what the results are, causal analysis is not appropriate. Leave such jobs under your old system, whatever it is. But if you can define the jobs' results and if they meet the criteria of linking up to eventual operating values and providing a product or service to customers and clients, build a micromap system of evaluation around the jobs.

5. *Develop a procedure for conducting an organic inquiry into the causes of results.* Such an inquiry is not difficult for critical incidents, which lend themselves to causal analysis because the time span is short enough to permit rigorous analysis. Longer accounts are more difficult. Even so, it is necessary to make at least gross judgments as to the effects of a manager's policy or program on results on a long-term basis.

The rules of inquiry gradually will become clear with experience through negotiation. Some very simple rules have been proposed: letting the person speak for himself or herself by volunteering an account of his or her own performance; and having the results evaluated by qualified others who distinguish carefully between Area 7 (action, effort, costs) and Area 8 (outcomes, visible results). We would be the first to say that these general principles are only a beginning.

6. *Train supervisors to use the entire micromap.* Many separate judging skills are involved. The skills appropriate to Area 1 include judging talent as in an interview (see Project 8), judging role consensus (see Chapter 5), and periodically checking feedback loops which might interfere with productivity (for example, Area 10–6). In most of these, the observer must get the help of the performer.

Training supervisors in micromap skills must include training in providing incentives to the performer to collaborate. This is one reason that we have used the term "negotiation" so often.

HIRING FOR RESULTS

Every method of hiring has come under scrutiny since EEO laws were enacted, and every method is in legal trouble. However, earlier they often were in *scientific* trouble for lack of validity. By validity we mean very simply that the hiring method obtains people who perform well on the job. If a method of hiring is not valid in this sense, it is not economic. In this way, if hiring methods are reshaped toward valid purposes, EEO pressures may ultimately affect business favorably.

As tests increasingly have been withdrawn from use, only two major methods remain: the application blank, which is legal but is steadily being cut down as its questions raise doubts; and the interview. But the traditional interview is perhaps the least reliable and least valid of all methods.

We nevertheless argue for using the interview as the centerpiece method, on ethical rather than scientific grounds. Employees and employers alike agree on its necessity. No one wants to be deprived of a right without a hearing; every applicant has a right to an interview. And no employer wants to hire anyone sight unseen.

The traditional interview presents a number of serious problems. One is its vagueness of purpose. The interview settled for impressionistic ratings; we insist that it obtain *evidence.* The vagueness permitted interviewers who thought they were rating well-defined traits to be influenced instead by "social merit." Such "merit" consists of the advantages most readers of this book have received from nature, family, or society. Even if you've earned your advantages, you must reorient your hiring system toward appraising performance merit, not social merit. Build your team around ugly uneducated quarterbacks who can pass rather than around men of distinction who can't. It is true that a person possessing social merit may also perform well. To insist on hiring for results is hardly making a case for reverse discrimination.

A general principle is that evidence of past working results is the best evidence for future working results. (We use that principle to reshape promotion as well, as in Projects 10 to 12). According to the principle that people have the right to present evidence about their own candidacies and, in short, to influence decisions about their vital life interests such as jobs, we have designed a type of structured interview which may be closer to an "interrogation" than to an interview. Since however, we do not want to lose the flexibility of the interview even though we seek more structure, perhaps the term "inquiry" is an appropriate compromise. The track record inquiry procedure is an organized conversation designed to help a person tell the story of past experiences which show his or her qualifications. It is up to you to decide how to evaluate what you hear.

The specific projects recommended are as follows:

7. *Survey the uses of social merit and demerit which are now prevalent among your hiring authorities.* Appearance, dress, speech, education, background (other than the track record of on-the-job results), and income influence hiring decisions. Even if they are free of legal liabilities (and some are suspicious), they are not the same as the applicant's track record of performance results. You should find out how much hiring decisions are influenced by social merit.

Whether or not you agree that few social criteria are job-relevant, at least you need an accurate reading of what is now influencing judgment in hiring. You can then decide the extent of your problem of moving to a results-oriented hiring system.

8. *Redesign the hiring interview for every position for which past-performance results are a reasonable requirement.* Critical incidents collected from present performers, if evaluated by qualified observers, can determine whether tangible results are expected in those jobs and what they are. These are used to lay out the structure of the hiring interview. The track record inquiry then shows a

Figure
10-2

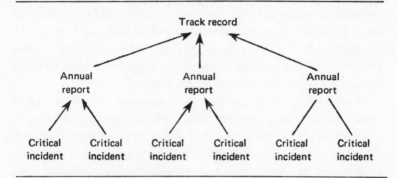

candidate how to advocate his or her own qualifications by defining the results expected and gives the candidate "air time" to do so.

9. Train everyone who hires to use such a structured inquiry. In practice, we have found that most managers consider a structured inquiry a sensible procedure. They can learn to start handling it within a day. As part of the training, however, you must make managers aware of the kinds of social merit or irrelevant credentials which we are all prone to overvalue. That is, the TRI which delivers results as evidence is useless if managers then ignore those results and look for the same social merit as in the past.

PROMOTING FOR RESULTS

Promotions should be based on working accounts. Recall that there is a hierarchy of such accounts, from brief to very long, as shown in Figure 10–2. These accounts can be proposed by the performers or developed by the person supervising them, or both. There is no obvious reason that people cannot volunteer evidence on their own behalf, especially since personnel dossiers have traditionally permitted others' impressions to be included.

Promotion accounts, however, would run into entrenched systems of politics, bureaucracy, psychological traits, and "good conduct." To the extent that these systems interfere with human performance and development, the case can be made for eliminating them. However, the power of custom and, indeed, the necessity of these entrenched systems (since they do have some business function) are such that a stronger case can be made for *integrating* them in the proposed promotion-for-results system.

Many companies believe that they now have a results-oriented system because they promote people whose operating results are good. However, financial outcomes and other operating records are not track records. The distinction is that such operating outcomes cannot explain themselves, and an individual's profit and loss statements may be due to his or her boss's decisions, not to his or her own. When an operating report is prepared so that the causes of the outcomes are known and are properly attributed to the performer, you have a working account useful for promotion.

It is apparent that opposition to a track record system will be considerable in some companies. While the opposing arguments have some weight, none is sufficiently heavy to overcome the bad effects of promoting nonperformers.

What specific projects are proposed?

10. *Survey the extent and strength of competing promotional systems.* This project would survey who gets promoted and why. Politics, bureaucracy, psychological traits, "good conduct," and operating results are among the reasons for promotion. By "strength" we mean the extent to which managers derive some benefit or feel some incentive to retain these systems. For example, a person who has made it through the political system may not think it so bad, because it has rewarded him or her. However, the person may also see costs being paid in the form of low morale and poor performance because favoritism is thought to be rife.

11. *Train potential candidates in self-advocacy.* Many companies are familiar with the benefits of posting jobs to open up more opportunities to more people. Job-posting programs inhibit clique formation and reduce the impression that insiders get favors. They

need to go further and give people practical help or training in using influence on their own behalf.

Does this sound like assertive training? Such broad self-advocacy is not intended here. The self-advocacy which is part of a promotion-for-results program is concerned more with working accounts. A person needs help in both writing and presenting accounts. Skill in such self-advocacy is not to be equated with "selling oneself." Rather, it is assertive self-advocacy based on operating effectiveness. People call their records forcefully to the attention of upper-level management.

12. *Develop a system of trained panels for appraising candidates for promotion.* Promotion decisions are usually influenced by the future superior. While this system has advantages we don't want to lose, we propose that you train these decision makers in the analysis of working accounts. The training should not be difficult. Moreover, seasoned managers don't resist the idea of working accounts; after all, these accounts describe the business and its operation. You need an overall system for selecting panels, preparing them for the task, notifying candidates, allowing candidates to update their records, verifying the records when necessary, and conducting the panel evaluation process itself.

Not least among the benefits of such a system should come in counseling the near-misses who did not quite get promoted. In the past, such counseling was often a charade. Instead of counseling, companies provided a confidence game in which the unsuccessful candidates in a highly politicized decision were persuaded that they had lost out because of some personal shortcoming which they should consider carefully. Such counseling is a cruel joke in which a weak, unjust, and operationally irrelevant promotion system is made to appear rational.

INCREASE THE VALUES GIVEN EXPERIENCE

Business has paid much lip service to "experience." This practice can be ended by taking experience seriously enough to learn what the term means. Two kinds of values are involved. One is that seasoned persons should be more precisely valued so that in later life they receive opportunities which use their experience. The other is that every manager should learn how to value his or her experience more highly.

Those who advocate credit for seniority give us clues to the value of experience. Experience means more than seniority, but that is a good place to begin. We find that:

- Experience refers both to what goes into a person and to what issues from that person: seasoned or expert performance.

- Experience has both a functional side (what was done) and an emotional side (what was ventured).

In taking an inventory of experience in this richer way, that is, in preparing an extended working account covering many years, the manager will learn that his or her assets are increasing. The inventory thus leads to an awareness of unused assets, which, then being more accessible, are available and usable. In that sense, the manager's assets have increased.

"Inventory taking" increases such assets because, by the very nature of management, insights result from comparing any result with its action. This is true for long time spans as well as for short ones. A manager, by reconstructing the way in which a project has gone since he or she initiated it several years ago, can learn lessons and add to his or her resources.

Thus the assets of experience are the one type of asset which age can increase. Among them is the analysis of failure. Defeats develop endurance to a greater degree than success does. Knowing what you have been able to endure in the past provides a good index of what you can take in the future. In short, managers can be helped to learn more from experience, thus deriving a second profit from it.

The specific projects which might be undertaken along these lines are as follows:

13. *Increase your use of seasoned people.* This does not mean to

hire greater numbers of older people because seasoning does not mean "older people."

A 25-year-old person who thinks his or her experience through fully may have more experience than a 35-year-old manager who lives in the present and never compares results with actions. However, the 35-year-old has *more* experience to make assets from.

We suspect that your company has major unused resources in the heads of its seasoned people. It would be good to inventory these resources and find ways to put them to profitable use. You should learn what seasoning does to your managers and determine in what ways experience is an asset. Learn how the subtler forms of experience—results, ventures, and values—are being obtained by managers and how they shape competence which your company could tap but does not. Business executives often say that their chief asset is their experience. We should find out whether and in what ways this is true.

14. *Learn to credit the emotional side of experience as well as the functional.* When you evaluate managers' candidacies, you should evaluate what they have ventured, endured, and valued as well as what they have accomplished and now know how to do. These features of experience are uncovered through the analysis of working accounts.

15. *Do this for yourself.* You can prepare your own working account (preferably lifelong) and take an inventory of your experience. If the entire track record is too much to digest, try an account of the past year. If you are not ready for that, try critical incidents of recent weeks or months. Whatever your time span, we see managerial self-knowledge as based primarily on knowledge of experience. If you find this review valuable to yourself, then why is it not valuable, at the right time, for every manager?

BIBLIOGRAPHY

Berlew, David, and Roger Harrison. Personal communication, 1976.

Bradford, J. Allyn, and Reuben Guberman. *Transactional awareness: Now I've got you in business.* Boston: Addison-Wesley, 1978.

Bray, Douglas, and Donald L. Grant. The assessment center in the measurement of potential for business management. *Psychol. Monogr.,* 1966, *80,* No. 17.

Dailey, Charles A. *Assessment of lives.* San Francisco: Jossey-Bass, 1971.

—*Entrepreneurial management.* New York: McGraw Hill, 1971.

Fivars, G. *Annotated bibliography of critical incident research.* Pittsburgh: American Institute for Research, 1971.

Flanagan, John. The critical incident technique. *Psychol. Bull.,* 1954, *51,* 327-350.

Heider, Fritz. *The psychology of interpersonal relations.* New York: Wiley, 1958.

Homans, George Caspar. *Social behavior.* New York: Harcourt Brace Jovanovich, 1974.

Jaques, Elliott. *Measurement of responsibility.* New York: Wiley, 1972.

Korzybski, Alfred. *Science and sanity.* Lancaster, Pa.: International Non-Aristotelian Library Publishing Co., 1933.

Lawler, Edward E. *Motivation in work organizations.* Monterey, Calif.: Brooks/Cole, 1973.

Lehman, H. C. *Age and achievement.* Princeton, N.J.: Princeton, 1953.

McCall, Morgan, Jr., and David L. DeVries. *Appraisal in context.* Greensboro, N.C.: Center for Creative Leadership, 1976.

McIntyre, James. Personal communication, 1976.

Malouf, Leroy. Personal communication, 1977.

Michaelson, George. Maggie Kuhn: Gray Panther on the Prowl, *Parade,* Dec. 18, 1977, 7–8.

Mintzberg, Henry. *The nature of managerial work.* New York: Harper & Row, 1973.

Mischel, W. *Personality and assessment.* New York: Wiley, 1968.

Odiorne, George, and Edwin Miller. Selection by objective. *Management of Personnel Quarterly,* Univer. of Michigan, 1966, 5, No. 3.

Polanyi, M. *Personal knowledge.* Chicago: Univer. of Chicago Press, 1958.

Sullivan, William, and Richard Meyers. *A guide for performance appraisal.* Wellesley, Mass.: Executive Development Center, 1976.

Vaccaro, A. J. *Performance appraisal.* Deerfield, Ill.: Travenol Laboratories, 1976.

Vroom, Victor. Organizational choice: A study of pre- and post-decision processes. *Organizational behavior and human performance,* 1966, 212–225.

Warr, Peter B., and Christopher Knapper. *The perception of people and events.* New York: Wiley, 1968.

INDEX